the
barbecue
cookbook

Published by Fog City Press
814 Montgomery Street
San Francisco, CA 94133 USA

Copyright © 2000 Weldon Owen Pty Ltd

Chief Executive Officer: John Owen
President: Terry Newell
Publisher: Sheena Coupe
Associate Publisher: Lynn Humphries
Senior Designer: Kylie Mulquin
Editorial Coordinator: Tracey Jackson
Production Managers: Helen Creeke, Caroline Webber
Production Assistant: Kylie Lawson
Business Manager: Emily Jahn
Vice President International Sales: Stuart Laurence

Project Editor: Lynn Cole
Designer: Jacqueline Richards

A catalog record for this book is available from the
Library of Congress, Washington, DC.

ISBN 1 875137 72 6

Color reproduction by Bright Arts Graphics (S) Pte Ltd
Printed by Toppan Printing Co, (H.K.) Ltd
Printed in China

A Weldon Owen Production

the
barbecue
cookbook

FOG CITY PRESS

contents

barbecue basics

recipes

barbecue basics

Some outdoor grills now look like close cousins of the kitchen stove. They make it possible to add succulent roasts, spicy curries, casseroles and seafood to your barbecue menus—even those old favorites, steaks, sausages and chops, stand a better chance of being cooked well. Mastering the art of barbecue cooking isn't hard. Choose the grill type that suits you best, then follow the basic rules that will lead to success.

basic equipment

It's not necessary to have a lot of special equipment for cooking a barbecue, but some items make the job easier and safer. Start with a heavy-duty apron and long matches or tapers for lighting up. Invest in some long-handled tongs—one set to move hot coals and wood around, the other to turn food. Long oven mitts protect arms and hands. A water spray is good for dousing flare-ups on solid-fuel grills but never spray water on a gas grill—move the food away from the flame and make a mental note to clean the lava before you use it again. Scrapers and cleaning brushes are essential. Small items of food are more manageable if threaded on skewers and you'll need a spatula to lift delicate items—some have a serrated edge to get under the food. With a hinged basket that holds fish or several chops or sausages at a time, it's easy to turn them all over together. Sturdy brushes are good for basting food during cooking and large salt and pepper shakers with handles are a boon to the cook.

types of grills

When you buy an outdoor grill, study the manufacturer's instructions carefully—different models require specific know-how to get the best out of them. Here, we outline the basics.

portable grills

A simple construction, the grate holds the fuel—usually charcoal. (The best known is the hibachi—the Japanese word for firebowl.) The food is cooked on a grill rack positioned above the hot coals. In some cases, the grill rack can be raised or lowered. Look for a sturdy model on solid legs so there's less danger of it tipping over. Air vents will make it easier to control the cooking heat and handles that don't get hot will be handy if you want to move your grill for any reason before the fire cools.

gas and electric grills

Volcanic lava rock, ceramic briquets or metal bars are heated by a gas flame or electric element. The temperature can be set and adjusted easily. Gas models are quick and particularly good if you decide to have a barbecue at short notice; they can be ready to cook in less than 10 minutes. Look for sturdy construction in a gas or electric grill and two or more heating zones. A built-in thermometer removes some of the guesswork and a tight-fitting lid allows you added versatility in cooking methods. Some models can be fitted with a rotisserie and smoking box as optional extras.

wood-fueled grills

These are usually table-type grills custom-built in your backyard or are the type you find in recreation parks and at communal functions. When the wood has burned down to glowing coals, the grill is ready to use. The cooking surface is either a solid plate or a grill rack, sometimes both.

covered, kettle-type or turbo grills

All the types of grill previously discussed are suitable for steaks, sausages, burgers, kabobs and all small, flat cuts of meat. But if you want to cook large cuts by the indirect heat method, a covered kettle-type grill is essential. These can be round or square. The heat is controlled by vents on the bottom as well as on the lid. These grills produce such wonderful roasts that you'll wonder why you ever bothered with a conventional kitchen oven. They can also be used for smoking.

roasting

A boon for the busy cook, kettle-type grills require very little preparation and the roast can be left to cook virtually by itself.

preparation tips

• Allow grill to heat with the lid off. The heat intensity is too severe when first lit, so wait for the coals to turn white before you start cooking. This will take about an hour so allow for this in your schedule. Rake hot coals to the sides of the grill, around a foil drip pan placed in the center of the grill for indirect cooking heat.

• To maximize tenderness, remove small roasts from the refrigerator 15 minutes prior to cooking. For larger roasts, allow 30 minutes.

• Trim excess fat from meat to prevent spatter and flare-ups. Position meat directly over the foil pan to catch drips.

• To keep meat moist throughout cooking and to add flavor, brush with a baste.

cooking tips

• Roast meat with the lid on and the vent open for the calculated time, basting occasionally with pan juices or a marinade.

• Remove roast from kettle-type grill. Cover and leave to rest in a warm place before carving. Resting keeps roasts juicy. Allow about 10 minutes for small roasts and 20 minutes for larger ones.

roasting times

Allow 7–8 minutes cooking time per 4 oz/125 g for small roasts weighing 3/4 lb–1 lb/400–500g; total 25–30 minutes.

For larger roasts 1 1/2–2 lb/750g–1kg, allow 25–30 minutes per 500g; total 45–60 minutes.

simple steps to
perfectly grilled meat, chicken and fish

sausages

• Sausages should not be pricked when cooking. (They'll burst and the juices will cause flare-ups. Also, they'll shrivel and become dry.) The secret to super, non-exploding sausages is to cook them slowly on the coolest section of the grill. Thick sausages will take 15–20 minutes.

• To shorten grilling time and to remove fat, partly cook sausages by placing them in a saucepan of cold water and bringing them to the boil briefly over moderate heat.

steak

• Trim meat of any excess fat. This reduces your fat intake and helps avoid flare-ups as the meat cooks. Nick the edges, particularly of thinner steaks, to prevent meat from curling during cooking.

• Don't season meat with salt before cooking; salt draws out the essential juices that keep it moist—you hardly want a dry, tough result.

• Marinate your steak. This helps tenderize the less-expensive cuts, and produces a wonderful flavor. When possible, marinate overnight to allow flavors to develop. An hour will be sufficient if you're in a hurry.

• Make sure the grill is well heated, but remember, you want heat to cook the meat, not flame. Charcoal or wood grills should be allowed to burn down to glowing coals.

• Drain meat from marinade; place on grill. Cook until well sealed, about 2–3 minutes on each side. For a rare steak, remove and serve. For a medium result, reduce heat to medium (gas or electric grill) or move

meat to a cooler part of a charcoal or wood grill. Cook until slightly springy to the touch, a further 2–3 minutes each side (a total of 4–6 minutes each side). For well-done steak continue cooking for a further 4–6 minutes each side (a total of 6–9 minutes each side). To lock in the juices that keep the meat moist and tender, don't turn it too often—three times will be plenty.

• Don't test for doneness during cooking by piercing meat with a fork or cutting with a knife or you'll lose the precious juices. To test, press the meat with blunt tongs: a rare result will be springy, medium a little firmer and well done will be very firm.

chicken and fish

• Skinless breast fillets are the easiest cut to grill. Marinate to give them more flavor and baste with oil during cooking to stop them drying out. For those attractive cross-hatched grill marks, place fillets on hot grill rack for 2 minutes. Using

tongs, rotate breasts 90° and grill for 2–4 minutes longer.

• To grill a large whole fish, place lemon slices and herbs in the body cavity and wrap fish in oiled aluminum foil. Cook over direct heat on the grill.

kabobs and satays

• Select lean meat and trim off any visible fat. Cut meat evenly into 1-in/2.5-cm cubes for kabobs or thin strips for satays. (For a quicker start, buy the meat ready prepared and marinated from the butcher.)

• Use bamboo or metal skewers, preferably with wooden handles. Bamboo skewers must be soaked in water for about 30 minutes before use to prevent charring. Soaking also helps stop meat from falling off or rolling over while cooking; the wood swells when immersed in water and will shrink at the same rate as the food when it is cooking. Metal skewers can simply be oiled to make it easy to remove the cooked meat.

• For straight metal skewers, compact the meat (and vegetables, if using) to prevent the food going rollabout. Closely packed ingredients take a little longer to cook.

• Cooking times are approximate and will vary according to the cut of the meat, its thickness, how tightly packed it is on the skewers and the type of grill.
Rare: Kabobs, 2–3 minutes each side. Satays, 1–2 minutes each side.
Medium: Kabobs, 4–6 minutes each side. Satays, 2–3 minutes each side.
Well done: Kabobs, 6–9 minutes each side. Satays, 3–4 minutes each side.

fueling your
grill

There are many different types of grill fuel available. Purists maintain that there is simply no substitute for wood; charcoal enthusiasts extol its virtues; advocates of the heat bead or briquet praise the enduring heat; gas fans love its instant response. The truth is that no one fuel is better than the other. Each has its advantages and each gives good results, provided it is used properly.

gas

Most gas grills have two or more burners with independent controls, which makes them very economical—you don't have to heat up the entire cooking area for just a few chops. The food is not cooked by the gas flames but by radiated heat. Some models use metal bars coated with porcelain or vitreous enamel to distribute the heat but the more usual material is chunks of natural lava or compressed lava compounds. Meat juices and fats falling on the hot distributor create steam and smoke that fill the air with the familiar barbecue smell and impart that special flavor to the food. Frequent flare-ups indicate that the distributor needs cleaning. (Always give your grill plate a good scrape as you heat it, to remove anything left from the last time you used it. After the barbecue, soak the cooled lava overnight in a bucket of hot water and dishwasher detergent, rinse thoroughly under running water and leave it out in the sun to dry.)

wood

Aficionados of wood for grilling often have a favorite. Different woods give distinctly different flavors. Hickory and mesquite are universally popular, but vine prunings, fruit wood and oak are all suitable for cooking. More resinous woods, such as pine and eucalypts, can impart a bitter taste to the food. Never use old building materials—wood that has been painted or treated can give off poisonous fumes.

For best results, your wood must be quite dry; green or wet wood won't burn properly. Firelighters should not be necessary—just some scrunched-up paper, twigs for kindling and then the larger pieces of wood. Position the fire where the breeze can flow through; the flames should flare up and quickly die down to form embers. Wait until there is a bed of glowing embers before heating the grill or hotplate and don't put the food on until all the flames have died down. If there are flames, the meat will be singed on the outside and raw in the center.

smoking

For a lovely smoky flavor, make "logs" of your chosen wood by wrapping chips, pre-soaked in water, in foil. Place the foil "log" on the hot fuel or lava and wait for 10 minutes or so until it begins to smolder and smoke. A log made with about 4 oz/125 g wood chips should go on smoking for a good half-hour. This method is especially effective in a covered grill. The woody stems of herbs can also add another dimension to the flavor of your grill.

This recipe, Leg of Lamb with Couscous, has been cooked using mesquite or hickory as a fuel. This gives it a distinctly smoky flavor (recipe page 18).

steps for
lighting charcoal

◀ one

Lighting Charcoal Arrange the charcoal in a pyramid in the center of the lower grate. If it is self-lighting, ignite with a match. If not, use an electric starter or put three or four firelighters under the pile.

◀ two

Charcoal for Direct Heat Cooking Use long-handled tongs to spread the hot coals in a single layer across the grate. Food will cook more evenly if the coals are arranged with about 1/2 in/1 cm of space between each.

◀ three

Charcoal for Indirect Heat Cooking Arrange hot coals around edge of grate, leaving space in the center. Set a disposable foil drip pan in space, surrounded by charcoal. Place food on the upper cooking rack, over the drip pan; cover with the lid so the heat and smoke circulate evenly.

◀ four

Testing the Heat of the Coals Hold your hand, palm-side-down, at about the height at which food will cook. If you must pull your hand away after 2 seconds, coals are hot; 3 seconds, medium hot; 4 seconds, medium; 5 seconds, medium slow; 6 seconds, slow. With indirect heat, coals should be one level hotter over the drip pan than the temperature you want.

charcoal

Commercially produced by burning wood slowly without oxygen, charcoal burns cleaner, hotter and more efficiently than wood. While not free, it is readily available and easy to store (always keep it dry). You can also calculate how much you will need. Once it is glowing, it gives off excellent heat. If you want to save the charcoal for future use once the food is cooked, simply pour on water to extinguish the fire and dry out the coals to use again. Grilling over charcoal imparts a delicious wood-smoky flavor to foods.

On the downside, charcoal can be hard to light—you may have to use firelighters. Also, your fire may not last quite long enough to cook large pieces of meat. This problem can be easily overcome by burning heat beads along with the charcoal.

heat beads

Also known as briquets, heat beads are made of compressed charcoal or brown coal. Every brand is different, so try them out, then stick to the one you like best so that you get to know how the beads behave. Heat beads generally take a while to get going (firelighters are usually essential) but they also burn for a long time. A 6 lb/3 kg bag should give about 6 hours of cooking heat. This makes them ideal for marathon grilling sessions and large joints of meat but not so practical for seafood and cuts of meat that are cooked quickly.

firelighters

The safest and most controllable firelighters are the solid bar types. They look like milk ice blocks and are based on paraffin or petroleum. Place three or four blocks in the center of your grill and pile the charcoal over them. Firelighters give off fumes while they burn with a hot flame for about 15 minutes. Do not put grills or hotplates in place or start cooking until well after the firelighters have burned out. When the coals are glowing red, spread them over the grill in a single layer and put your grill rack or plate in position. Start cooking when the coals are covered with a gray-white ash and have reached the required temperature (*see Testing the Heat of the Coals, page 10*).

safety tips

• Never pour flammable liquids, such as paraffin or petroleum, on a fire to get it going as they will flare up dangerously.

• Make sure the grill is on a level surface and that there is no danger of it tipping over.

• Never leave a grill unattended.

• Store spare gas cylinders in a dry shed or garage, never under the grill or inside your house.

• Always start with a clean grill (see manufacturer's directions).

char-grilling

The key to successful char-grilling is probably patience. Don't be tempted to start cooking until your fire is just right. Get to know your grill—where its hottest spots are and how long it takes to reach the optimum temperature for a sizzling performance.

preparation tips

• Trim any excess fat from meat to prevent spatter and flare-ups. Marinate meat for at least 1 hour, or overnight if you have the time. The longer you marinate, the more intense the flavor will be. Remove meat from refrigerator 15 minutes prior to cooking to maximize tenderness. If desired, brush meat with remaining marinade to keep it moist during cooking and to give extra flavor.

char-grill basics

• Heat grill on high. (For wood or charcoal grills, heat to glowing coals. There must be no flames.) Place meat on grill and allow it to brown and seal well before turning over with tongs. The amount of time this takes will depend on the size and the thickness of the cut. As a general rule, when juices appear on the uncooked side of the meat, this is a good indication that it's time to turn.

• Cook other side of the meat until browned and sealed. It's important not to keep on turning the meat. Frequent turning doesn't seal the meat well enough to keep in the juices and it becomes dry and tough. For the same reason, don't pierce or cut the meat with a fork or knife.

• Cook until done to your liking. Test meat by pressing it with tongs.
Rare: Remove when sealed on both sides and the meat feels springy.
Medium: After sealing both sides, reduce heat to medium. If you are using a wood or charcoal grill, move the meat to a cooler section of the grill. Continue cooking until it feels a little firmer, turning it twice at most.
Well done: After sealing both sides, reduce heat to medium. If using wood or charcoal grills, move meat to a cooler section. Cook until meat feels firm, turning it twice only.

safety tips

• Use long-handled brushes for basting.

• Don't wear long-sleeved or loose clothing while cooking over a grill.

• Never put cooked meat on the same platter that the raw or marinated meat was on. The dangerous bacteria that cause food poisoning can multiply quickly in warm, moist situations.

• Take care to dispose of ashes safely—live coals remain a fire hazard for a surprisingly long time.

beef and lamb

Beef and lamb are the
traditional favorites at a
barbecue. Marinate your
chosen cut overnight and
you'll have the makings
of a delicious meal.

The recipes in this section look
good and taste great, and you'll
be pleasantly surprised at
how easy they are to cook.
Whether you're cooking
for a crowd or for just a few
people, there are plenty of
alternatives to suit your needs.

grilled lamb on skewers

2 small onions, grated

1 cup/8 fl oz/250 ml olive oil

1 teaspoon freshly ground black pepper

1 teaspoon dried oregano or
2 teaspoons fresh thyme

1 teaspoon ground cinnamon

1 teaspoon ground cumin

Pinch of ground red pepper flakes
(cayenne pepper) (optional)

2 lb/1 kg tender lamb from the leg, trimmed and
cut across the grain into 1½-in/4-cm cubes

1 red (Spanish) onion, cut into
1-in/2.5-cm squares

Salt

2 ripe but firm tomatoes, cored and halved

2 green bell peppers (capsicums), seeded, deribbed
and cut into 1½-in/4-cm squares

Yogurt-cucumber sauce (optional) (*see box below*)

In a non-aluminum bowl, combine onion, ¾ cup/6 fl oz/190 ml olive oil, black pepper, oregano or thyme, cinnamon, cumin and the red pepper flakes, if using. Stir to mix well, then add lamb cubes, turning to coat evenly. Cover and leave to marinate overnight in the refrigerator.

Prepare a fire in a grill. Remove lamb cubes from marinade, reserving marinade. Thread meat cubes onto metal skewers, alternating them with onion pieces. (Do not pack lamb and onion pieces too tightly or they will not cook evenly.) Brush lamb and onions with some of the remaining olive oil and sprinkle with salt and black pepper. Thread tomatoes and bell pepper squares on skewers, brushing with oil and sprinkling with salt and pepper.

Place lamb skewers on an oiled grill rack and grill, turning once and basting occasionally with reserved marinade, for 8–10 minutes total for medium-rare, or until meat is done to your liking. About 5 minutes before lamb is ready, place tomato and pepper skewers on grill rack and grill, turning as needed, for 5 minutes, or until tender when pierced with a knife.

Transfer skewers to a warmed serving dish or individual plates. Serve hot with yogurt-cucumber sauce in a bowl on the side.

SERVES 4–6

yogurt-cucumber sauce

Dice 2 Lebanese cucumbers finely and place in a sieve lined with cheesecloth (muslin). Sprinkle with salt and place over a bowl to drain for 30 minutes. Rinse. Combine with 1 cup/8 oz/250 g plain yogurt and 1 clove garlic, minced; season. Refrigerate, covered, until needed. Use within 2 days.

grilled veal chops
with salad

veal chops

4 veal loin chops with bone,
each about 8 oz/250 g

2 cloves garlic, cut in halves
lengthwise

Freshly ground pepper

4 teaspoons good-quality olive oil

salad

1 small bunch arugula (rocket),
stems removed

2 radicchio leaves, sliced into
thin shreds

4 Belgian endive (witloof/chicory)
leaves, sliced into thin shreds

2 small artichokes, fresh or frozen
and thawed, trimmed (optional)
(bottled artichokes can be used,
if preferred)

1 oz/30 g good-quality
Parmesan cheese

4 lemon wedges, to serve

Good-quality olive oil, to serve

Slash the fat along the edge of each veal chop in 3 places with a sharp knife to avoid curling during cooking. Place each chop between 2 sheets of plastic wrap (film) and pound with a meat mallet until about 1/2 in/1 cm thick. Rub each chop all over with half of a garlic clove, pepper to taste and 1 teaspoon of the olive oil. Let stand at room temperature for 1 hour.

Prepare a fire in a grill. Arrange chops on a grill rack and grill over hot coals, turning once, until done to your liking. For rare, cook 2–3 minutes on first side and 1–2 minutes on second; for medium, cook 4–5 minutes on first side and 3–4 minutes on second; for well done, cook 6–7 minutes on first side and 5–6 minutes on second.

Transfer chops to warmed individual plates and scatter an equal amount of arugula, radicchio and endive over the top of each chop. Thinly slice artichokes lengthwise, if using, and scatter over the salad. Using a sharp knife or vegetable peeler, shave off paper-thin slices of Parmesan cheese and scatter over greens. Place a lemon wedge on each plate and pass olive oil for drizzling over the top.

SERVES 4

indian spiced
lamb cutlets

3 teaspoons prepared
Madras curry paste

3 teaspoons prepared
korma curry paste

3 teaspoons prepared
tandoori curry paste

About 1³/₄ cups/14 oz/440 g
plain yogurt

12 lamb cutlets, with most of the
fat trimmed off

1 tablespoon chopped mint

Steamed rice, colored with
turmeric, to serve

 Combine each curry paste with about 3¹/₂ oz/110 g yogurt. Coat 4 cutlets with each of the flavored yogurts. Prepare a fire in a grill. Cook the cutlets on a rack over high heat for about 5 minutes. Turn over and grill the other side for 5 minutes more, or until done to your liking. Let stand in a warm place for 5 minutes to rest.

Meanwhile, combine remaining plain yogurt with mint. Serve 3 cutlets per person, one of each flavor, with steamed rice and minted yogurt. Accompany with a good Indian chutney, if liked.

SERVES 4

two simple sauces

pine nut sauce

Heat ¹/₂ tablespoon butter in a saucepan, add 2 oz/60 g pine nuts and cook until lightly golden. Remove from pan with a slotted spoon and place in food processor. Cook 1 medium onion, diced, in ¹/₂ tablespoon butter until lightly golden. Add 1¹/₄ cups/10 fl oz/310 ml apricot nectar and 2 teaspoons wholegrain mustard. Bring to the boil, simmer for 5 minutes. Add mixture to pine nuts in processor and process until smooth. Return sauce to pan and heat through over low heat. Season to taste and serve hot with lamb.

thai barbecue sauce

Heat 1 teaspoon canola oil in pan over high heat. Add 1-2 teaspoons green curry paste and fry until fragrant. Add 1 tablespoon chopped fresh cilantro (fresh coriander/Chinese parsley) leaves, 1 teaspoon Thai fish sauce and 1 cup/8 fl oz/ 250 ml coconut milk; stir well. Heat through and pour over sliced steak or kabobs.

spicy hamburgers

Combine onion and tomato slices in a small bowl with lemon juice and 3 tablespoons of the olive oil. Turn to coat evenly and set aside.

Prepare a fire in a grill. Combine meat, salt, pepper, chili sauce and ice water in a large bowl (the ice water helps to keep the burgers juicy). Stir with a fork until well mixed. Then, using your hands, form meat mixture into 4 patties each 1 in/2.5 cm thick, being careful not to handle the meat too much. Set aside.

Place onion rolls or hamburger buns, cut-side-down, on the grill rack and grill for 2–3 minutes, or until just golden. Transfer to individual plates, cut-side-up, and brush the remaining 1 tablespoon olive oil lightly over toasted buns.

Position the grill rack 4 in/10 cm from the heat source, then grill burgers, turning once, for 6 minutes on the first side and 4–5 minutes on the second side for medium-rare to medium.

Place each burger on the bottom half of the toasted bun, top with a slice each of red onion and tomato, and sprinkle with a little lettuce. Cover with the top bun. Serve at once.

SERVES 4

4 thick slices red (Spanish) onion

4 thick slices beefsteak tomato

1 1/2 tablespoons fresh lemon juice

1/3 cup/2 1/2 fl oz/80 ml olive oil

1 1/3 lb/660 g ground (minced) sirloin or chuck steak

1/2 teaspoon salt

1/4 teaspoon freshly ground pepper

1/4 cup/2 fl oz/60 ml bottled chili sauce

1/4 cup/2 fl oz/60 ml ice water

4 large onion rolls or hamburger buns, split

2 1/2 oz/75 g shredded iceberg lettuce

leg of lamb
with couscous

1 leg of lamb, about 8½ lb /4.25 kg, boned and butterflied (about 6½ lb/3.25 kg boned)

¼ cup/2 fl oz/60 ml good-quality olive oil

1 tablespoon chopped garlic

2 teaspoons salt

2 teaspoons freshly cracked pepper

1½ teaspoons chopped fresh rosemary

Grated zest (rind) and juice of 1 lemon

Fresh mint sprigs, for garnish

Place boned leg of lamb in a non-aluminum dish. Combine olive oil, garlic, salt, pepper, rosemary, lemon zest and juice in a small, shallow bowl. Drizzle mixture over lamb and rub it in well. Cover and refrigerate for 3–12 hours. About 1 hour before cooking, remove from refrigerator and bring to room temperature.

Prepare a fire in a grill using hardwood charcoal, such as mesquite or hickory. When coals have burned down to a gray ash, place lamb on grill rack with the outside of the leg facing down. Grill for about 10 minutes. Turn over and grill for about 10 minutes longer for medium-rare, or until dark brown and done to your liking. Transfer to a large platter to rest for 5 minutes.

Thinly slice lamb across the grain and arrange on individual plates along with a mound of the couscous (*recipe in box left*). Garnish with a mint sprig and serve.

SERVES 8

couscous

Place 4 cups/1¾ lb/875 g couscous in a heatproof bowl. Combine 4 cups/1 qt/1 l chicken stock or water with 4 oz/125 g diced red bell pepper (capsicum), 1 teaspoon saffron threads, 1 teaspoon chopped garlic and 1 teaspoon salt in a small saucepan and bring to a boil over high heat. Pour over couscous, stir to combine and cover with plastic wrap (film). Let stand for 8 minutes. Fluff with a fork to break the couscous into individual grains. Let rest 5 minutes longer. Add 1 oz/30 g chopped green (spring) onions, 2 oz/60 g dried currants, 1½ oz/45 g toasted pine nuts, 1 tablespoon chopped fresh mint, 2 tablespoons olive oil and toss well to combine.

Serve at room temperature or reheat briefly in a non-stick frying pan over high heat, tossing often, for 1–2 minutes.

thai beef salad

About 2 lb/1 kg beef fillet

1 tablespoon prepared lime and chili sauce

2 teaspoons fish sauce

1 tablespoon sesame oil

2 tablespoons lime juice

2 tablespoons chopped fresh cilantro (fresh coriander/Chinese parsley) or mint leaves

About 4 oz/125 g mixed salad leaves

4 oz/125 g cherry tomatoes

1 red (Spanish) onion, sliced

2 fresh mangoes, peeled, pitted and sliced

 Prepare a fire in a grill and cook beef over high heat for 4–5 minutes on each side, or until done to your liking (8–10 minutes for rare; 10–12 minutes for medium rare; 12–15 minutes for well done). Let stand in a warm place for 5 minutes to rest.

Combine lime and chili sauce with fish sauce, sesame oil, lime juice and cilantro. Toss salad leaves in a bowl with cherry tomatoes and onion. Pour over dressing and toss again. Arrange slices of mango and thinly sliced beef over the top. Serve salad with crusty bread, if desired.

SERVES 4

barbecued roast
with bell pepper dill sauce

1 boneless leg of lamb
or 1 beef fillet,
about 1 lb/500 g

bell pepper
dill sauce

1 medium red bell pepper
(capsicum), chopped

1/4 cup/2 fl oz/60 ml sweet
white wine

2 teaspoons chopped
fresh dill

Freshly ground black pepper,
to taste

 Prepare a fire in a kettle-type grill. Cook roast, with indirect heat, according to grill manufacturer's instructions, over a drip tray for 25–30 minutes.

For sauce, microwave bell pepper and 1 tablespoon wine in a microwave-proof dish, covered, on High (100% power) for 6–8 minutes. Process bell pepper and remaining wine in a food processor. Add dill and black pepper.

When roast is cooked, remove from grill and rest, covered, for 5–10 minutes. The meat will retain its juices and 'firm up' a little, making it easier to carve. Serve sliced with sauce and Almond Rice Salad (*see recipe below*).

SERVES 2

almond rice
salad

1/2 cup/3 oz/90 g quick-
cooking brown rice

2 tablespoons
flaked almonds

3 oz/90 g celery,
finely chopped

3 oz/90 g sultanas

 Cook rice according to instructions on the packet. Place almonds in a microwave-proof dish and toast, stirring occasionally, in a microwave oven on High (100% power) for 2 minutes. Combine rice, almonds, celery and sultanas in a serving bowl.

SERVES 2

flavored butters

Add interesting flavor notes to simple grilled meats with one of these delicious butters. Each recipe makes about 10 oz/315 g. These flavored, or compound, butters will keep for 4 days in the refrigerator and about 1 month in the freezer.

herb and lime butter

Serve with meat, fish or poultry.

Process 8 oz/250 g softened butter with 1 tablespoon grated lime zest (rind), 2 tablespoons lime juice, 1 clove garlic, minced, 2 shallots, minced, 1 tablespoon chopped tarragon and 2 tablespoons each chopped parsley and chopped chives in a food processor until combined. Spoon mixture into a serving dish and refrigerate until firm.

mustard and horseradish butter

Serve with red meats.

Process 8 oz/250 g softened butter with 1 clove garlic, minced, 2 tablespoons grain mustard, 1 tablespoon prepared horseradish, 2 tablespoons chopped chives and 1 tablespoon chopped fresh rosemary in a food processor until combined. Spoon mixture into a serving dish and refrigerate until firm.

chili-ginger butter

Serve with meat, fish or poultry.

Process 8 oz/250 g softened butter with 1 clove garlic, minced, 2 teaspoons chili oil, 1 teaspoon chopped fresh chili, 1 tablespoon grated fresh ginger root, 2 teaspoons paprika and 1 tablespoon tomato paste in a food processor until combined. Spoon mixture into a serving dish and refrigerate until firm.

grilled meatballs
with yogurt sauce and onion salad

2 lb/1 kg ground (minced) lean beef

2 yellow or red (Spanish) onions, grated (about 7½ oz/235 g)

2 cloves garlic, finely minced

2 eggs, lightly beaten

1 tablespoon chopped fresh thyme

1 teaspoon freshly ground pepper

½ teaspoon salt, plus salt to taste

Olive oil, for brushing

6 pita breads, warmed, to serve

Sliced tomato, to serve (optional)

Prepare a fire in a grill.

Combine beef in a bowl with grated onion, garlic, eggs, thyme, pepper and ½ teaspoon salt. Mix with your hands until mixture holds together well. Form into 12 ovals about 3 in/7.5 cm long and 1½ in/4 cm wide and thread them onto metal skewers. Brush meatballs with olive oil and sprinkle with salt. Place skewers on an oiled grill rack and grill, turning to brown on all sides, for about 8 minutes, or until cooked through.

Remove skewers from grill and slip meatballs off skewers. Cut pita breads into halves and tuck a meatball into each half. Serve at once. Pass sliced tomato, yogurt sauce and onion salad (*recipes in box below right*) at the table for guests to add to taste.

SERVES 6

tandoori lamb

1¹/₂ tablespoons prepared tandoori curry paste

About 8 oz/250 g plain yogurt

1 leg of lamb, about 2 lb/1 kg

Salad vegetables or steamed rice, flavored with turmeric, to serve

 Combine tandoori paste with about 6 oz/185 g yogurt. Coat lamb with mixture and set aside to marinate for about 1 hour so flavors will develop.

Prepare a fire in a kettle-type grill. Place lamb in a pan and add about a cup of water to stop the juices from burning. Cook meat, covered, over indirect heat, following the grill manufacturer's instructions and basting frequently with marinade, for 40–70 minutes, or until done to your liking (for each 1 lb/500 g allow about 20–25 minutes for rare; 25–30 minutes for medium rare; 30–35 minutes for well done). Let stand in a warm place for 15 minutes to rest. Carve and serve with the remaining plain yogurt and saffron rice, if liked.

SERVES 4

yogurt sauce

Line a large sieve with cheesecloth (muslin), place sieve over a bowl and spoon 4 cups/2 lb/1 kg plain yogurt into sieve. Refrigerate for 4–6 hours to drain off excess water. You should have 1¹/₂ –2 cups/12–16 oz/375–500 g drained yogurt. Add 3 large cloves garlic, finely minced, ¹/₄ cup/2 fl oz/60 ml olive oil and 1 tablespoon red wine vinegar or fresh lemon juice to the drained yogurt. Stir well and fold in 1 tablespoon chopped fresh mint. Season to taste with salt and pepper. Cover and refrigerate until needed.

onion salad

Thinly slice 1 lb/500 g red (Spanish) or white onions. Place in a large sieve or colander, add 1 tablespoon salt and toss well. Let stand for 15 minutes. Rinse onion slices with cool water and pat dry with paper towels. Place in a bowl and add 3 tablespoons chopped fresh flat-leaf (Italian) parsley and 1 teaspoon sumac (a Middle Eastern spice). Toss well and set aside.

steak and salad
in roll-ups

It doesn't take much effort to turn a grilled steak into something that little bit special. Flatbreads—pita bread pockets from the Middle East, lavash bread from Eastern Europe and naan from India—are available in specialty supermarkets and delicatessens. Used as pockets or wrap-arounds for sliced meat and other ingredients, they are great for casual meals. Prepare them and eat them hot, or cook the meat in advance and make up the 'parcels' for a picnic. They're easily transported. Tortillas and crispy Mexican tacos can be used as containers for meat and salad in the same way.

Dice grilled steak and mix with chopped salad greens or tabbouleh, cucumber and green (spring) onions. Stir through a salad dressing of your choice. Wrap in lavash bread, or pile into pita bread pockets.

chili lamb kabobs

Process onion, garlic, chilies, coconut, 2 tablespoons of the juice and 1 tablespoon of the soy sauce in a food processor to a thickish paste.

Place meat in a large dish and stir the onion mixture through; leave to marinate in a cool place for 10 minutes.

Prepare a fire in a grill to a high heat. Thread the lamb onto oiled skewers. Cook, turning occasionally, for 8–10 minutes, or until done to your liking.

Combine peanut butter, water and chili sauce in a small pan, stirring over medium heat until smooth. Remove from heat, stir in remaining juice and soy sauce.

Cook pappadums, 6 at a time, in a microwave oven on High (100% power) for 1 minute. (Do not use a convection-type microwave oven because arcing may occur.) Serve with kabobs and sauce.

SERVES 4–6

1 medium onion, roughly chopped

2 cloves garlic, peeled

1–2 medium red chilies, seeded

2 tablespoons flaked coconut

1/4 cup/2 fl oz/60 ml lemon juice

2 tablespoons soy sauce

1 1/2 lb/750 g diced lean lamb

4 oz/125 g peanut butter (smooth or crunchy)

1/2 cup/4 fl oz/125 ml hot water

Few drops chili sauce (optional)

12–18 pappadums

oriental
beef sticks

Prepare a fire in a grill to a high heat. Push beef strips onto 8–12 oiled bamboo skewers.

Combine all remaining ingredients and brush over meat. Cook skewers for 3–4 minutes each side, brushing repeatedly with the spicy sauce.

If you like to add vegetables to your skewers, make sure the pieces are the same size as the meat. Button mushrooms and summer (baby) squash can be used whole. Fruit can work well (both for its color and flavor), but it must be firm, not overripe or soft. Onion is great on a kabob. Cook for a few minutes first by simmering in water or cooking for a minute in the microwave oven.

SERVES 4–6

1 1/2 lb/750 g lean beef strips

1/2 cup/4 fl oz/125 ml plum sauce

2 teaspoons soy sauce

1 clove garlic, minced

1/2 teaspoon grated fresh ginger root

1/4 teaspoon minced chili

spicy beef salad
with tomato and mint

1 lb/500 g beef tri-tip or sirloin steak, about 2 in/5 cm thick

2 cloves garlic

2 tablespoons finely chopped coriander root

1 teaspoon ground black pepper

1½ teaspoons sugar

2 tablespoons soy sauce

1 tablespoon Thai fish sauce

1 tablespoon peanut or corn oil

thai vinaigrette

2 cloves garlic, minced

2 fresh small red or green chilies, chopped

1½ tablespoons sugar

¼ cup/2 fl oz/60 ml Thai fish sauce

⅓ cup/2½ fl oz/80 ml fresh lime juice

salad

6 large red lettuce leaves

3 small, firm tomatoes, cut into wedges

1 small red (Spanish) onion, sliced

1 small cucumber, peeled and thinly sliced

8 fresh mint leaves, coarsely chopped

4 kaffir lime or other citrus leaves, very finely shredded (optional)

2 tablespoons chopped fresh cilantro (fresh coriander/ Chinese parsley) leaves, plus whole leaves for garnish

 Place beef in a bowl. Combine garlic, coriander, black pepper and sugar in a mortar and mash to a paste with a pestle. Stir in soy sauce, fish sauce and oil. Rub mixture into beef and let marinate for at least 1 hour at room temperature, or cover and refrigerate for up to 4 hours.

For vinaigrette, combine garlic and chilies in a mortar and mash to a paste with a pestle. Stir in sugar, fish sauce and lime juice. Set aside.

Prepare a fire in a grill. Place beef on grill rack and grill, turning once, for 5–8 minutes on each side, or until medium-rare. Remove from heat and let cool. Cut beef across the grain into very thin slices. Place in a large bowl. Add two-thirds of the vinaigrette and toss well to coat; set aside.

Just before serving, combine lettuce, torn or shredded, in a large bowl with tomatoes, onion, cucumber, chopped mint, lime or citrus leaves (if using) and chopped cilantro leaves. Drizzle with remaining vinaigrette, toss gently.

Divide evenly among 6 individual salad plates. Mound the beef mixture on top. Garnish with cilantro leaves. Serve warm or at room temperature.

SERVES 6

grilled rack of lamb
with ratatouille

Place lamb in a shallow non-aluminum container and rub all over with olive oil, garlic, rosemary, salt and pepper. Cover and refrigerate for 3–12 hours.

Heat olive oil over medium heat in a large saucepan or heavy frying pan. Add sliced onion and cook for about 5 minutes, or until translucent. Add garlic and continue to cook for 2–3 minutes longer. Add zucchini, eggplant and bell peppers and cook, stirring, until heated through, another 5 minutes. Add tomatoes, basil, salt and pepper and stir well. Cover, reduce heat to low and cook for about 30 minutes, or until tender.

Uncover the pan; the mixture should still be quite liquid. Cook for another 15–20 minutes, or until mixture thickens. Remove from heat, let cool briefly and stir in parsley. Set aside. (At this point, the ratatouille can be covered and refrigerated for up to 3 days; reheat when needed.)

Before ratatouille is done, prepare a fire in a grill using hardwood charcoal such as mesquite or hickory. When coals have burned down to a gray ash, place lamb on the grill rack with the rounded side of rack bones facing up. Cook for 6–8 minutes, turn over, cook for another 6–8 minutes, turn over one more time and cook for a final 2–3 minutes for medium rare. To check doneness, cut an incision into the underside of the lamb. There should still be some pinkness, but this is a matter of your preference. Transfer to a cutting board and let rest for 5 minutes in a warm spot. Cut rack into 2-bone portions and serve immediately with some of the ratatouille.

SERVES 4

1 rack of lamb with 8 chops, about 3 lb/1.5 kg, bones trimmed of fat

1/4 cup/2 fl oz/60 ml good-quality olive oil

1 tablespoon minced garlic

2 teaspoons coarsely chopped fresh rosemary

1 1/4 teaspoons salt

1/2 teaspoon freshly ground pepper

ratatouille

1/2 cup/4 fl oz/125 ml good-quality olive oil

7 oz/220 g yellow onions, sliced

3 cloves garlic, thinly sliced

3 zucchini (courgettes), cut crosswise into pieces about 1/2 in/1 cm thick

1 eggplant (aubergine), peeled and cut into slices about 1/2 in/1 cm thick

2 red bell peppers (capsicums), seeded, deribbed and cut into large pieces

15 oz/470 g diced plum (Roma) tomatoes

3 fresh basil sprigs, chopped

1 1/2 teaspoons salt

1/2 teaspoon freshly ground pepper

2 tablespoons chopped fresh flat-leaf (Italian) parsley

greek
lamb skewers

1 1/2 lb/750 g diced
lean lamb

1/4 cup/2 fl oz/60 ml
lemon juice

1 tablespoon olive oil

2 teaspoons
minced garlic

2 teaspoons chopped
fresh oregano leaves

Marinate diced lamb in combined lemon juice, oil, garlic and oregano for 1–12 hours.

Prepare a fire in a grill to a high heat. (For wood or charcoal barbecues, heat to glowing coals. There must be no flames.)

Thread diced lamb onto metal skewers, reserving marinade to use as a baste. Cook, turning and basting occasionally, for about 8 minutes, or until sealed, well browned and done to your liking.

SERVES 4

mini roasts

2 small boneless loin of
lamb roasts

1/4 cup/2 fl oz/60 ml
strained ginger
marmalade, or
marinade of
your choice

1 teaspoon
minced garlic

1 tablespoon soy sauce

Prepare a fire in a kettle-type grill. Allow to heat for at least 1 hour with the lid off.

Weigh roasts individually to calculate cooking time (based on weight of *one* roast only). Combine remaining ingredients and brush over surface of roasts.

Place lamb on grill rack. Cover and roast with vent open, brushing occasionally with soy mixture. For each 4 oz/125 g, allow 8–9 minutes for rare, 10–11 minutes for medium, or 12–13 minutes for well done.

Remove from grill. Leave to rest for 10 minutes in a warm place, covered loosely with foil.

SERVES 4

lamb satay

1¹/₂ kg/750 g diced lean lamb

¹/₄ cup/2 fl oz/60 ml soy sauce

2 tablespoons honey

1 tablespoon smooth peanut butter

1 teaspoon freshly chopped chilies

1 teaspoon minced garlic

Lemon wedges, to serve

Marinate lamb in combined soy sauce, honey, peanut butter, chili and garlic for 1–12 hours.

Preheat a fire in a grill to a high heat. (For wood or charcoal grills, heat to glowing coals. There must be no flames.)

Thread diced lamb on metal skewers, reserving marinade to use as a baste. Cook kabobs, turning and basting occasionally, for about 8 minutes, or until sealed, well browned and done to your liking. Serve with quick satay sauce (*see recipe in box below*).

SERVES 4

quick satay sauce

Combine 3 oz/90 g crunchy or smooth peanut butter with ¹/₃ cup/2¹/₂ fl oz/80 ml each of mild taco sauce and coconut cream in small pan and heat, stirring until smooth. Do not boil. Add a little water if sauce consistency is too thick. Serve hot with kabobs.

tasty meat marinades

To make any of these marinades, simply mix the ingredients thoroughly. Place meat in a glass or other non-aluminum dish, add marinade and turn meat to coat well. (Don't use a metal dish—acids will react with the metal, producing an unpleasant taste.) Store, covered, in the refrigerator for 2–12 hours. About 30 minutes before cooking, let meat come to room temperature. Drain meat before cooking. The remaining marinade can be used for basting the meat as it is cooking. These recipes make a quantity sufficient to marinate 4 servings of meat (1 serving is equivalent to 1 steak or 2 kabobs).

mediterranean

3 cloves garlic, minced

1/2 cup/4 oz/125 g tomato paste

1/2 cup/4 fl oz/125 ml olive oil

2 teaspoons dried oregano

1/4 cup/2 fl oz/60 ml red wine

horseradish

1 tablespoon canola oil

1 tablespoon horseradish cream

1/2 cup/4 fl oz/125 ml white wine

2 teaspoons chopped fresh cilantro (fresh coriander/Chinese parsley) leaves

2 teaspoons wholegrain mustard

honey mint

1/2 teaspoon sesame oil

1 tablespoon lemon juice

1/2–1 teaspoon seeded, minced chili

1 tablespoon chopped fresh mint leaves

2 teaspoons honey

orange teriyaki

Grated zest (rind) and juice of 1 orange

1/4 cup/2 fl oz/60 ml thick teriyaki baste

2 tablespoons soy sauce

1 tablespoon honey

spicy citrus

1 1/3 cups/11 fl oz/345 ml grapefruit juice

2/3 cup/5 fl oz/160 ml orange juice

2/3 cup/5 fl oz/160 ml olive oil (add a few drops sesame oil, optional)

2 teaspoons minced garlic

2 teaspoons hot paprika

2 tablespoons soft brown sugar or honey

spicy vindaloo paste

1 teaspoon ground cardamom

1 teaspoon seeded, minced chili

1 teaspoon ground cinnamon

2 teaspoons ground cumin

2 teaspoons turmeric

2 teaspoons hot mustard, smooth or grained

1/4 cup/2 fl oz/60 ml white vinegar

chinese

2 tablespoons honey

2 tablespoons dry sherry

2 tablespoons soy sauce

1 teaspoon sesame oil

1 teaspoon Chinese five spice powder

1 teaspoon minced garlic

1 teaspoon minced ginger

chili herbed roast
with roasted garlic

Prepare a fire in a kettle-type grill.

Cut a pocket through the length of the roast by running a sharp knife from one end to the other. Cut green onion to length of pocket and insert, along with mint leaves and garlic. Combine cilantro, chili sauce and oil in a large dish. Add meat and turn to coat in marinade. Leave in a cool place for 30 minutes.

Cook roast over drip tray, brushing with marinade throughout cooking, for 25–30 minutes. Rest, covered, for 5–10 minutes before carving.

SERVES 2

1 beef fillet or tenderloin, about 1 lb/500 g

1 green (spring) onion

4 fresh mint leaves

1 large clove garlic, peeled and quartered

1 tablespoon chopped fresh cilantro (fresh coriander/Chinese parsley) leaves

1 tablespoon sweet chili sauce

1 tablespoon canola oil

roasted garlic

Use large, whole bulbs (also known as heads) of garlic and slice them straight across the top (the pointed part), about a third of the way down. Brush cut surface with olive oil and place in a covered kettle-type grill on a moderate heat for about 15 minutes, or until garlic has softened. Insert the point of a skewer in one of the cloves to test if it is done; it should slip in easily. Allow to cool slightly and then simply squeeze out the garlicky paste from each clove. This process of cooking produces a very mellow flavor that is quite unlike the pungency of raw garlic. Serve whole as a vegetable or as a topping for grilled meat. Also delicious spread on crusty bread in place of butter.

glazed lamb
with bell pepper salsa

12 lamb cutlets or 4 lb/2 kg short ribs

1/3 cup/2 1/2 fl oz/80 ml teriyaki sauce

bell pepper salsa

2 tablespoons sunflower oil

1 medium onion, quartered

1 medium red bell pepper (capsicum), chopped

1 teaspoon minced garlic

13 oz/410 g can peeled tomatoes, roughly chopped

1 tablespoon balsamic vinegar

1 tablespoon maple syrup

1/4 teaspoon cracked black peppercorns

1/4 teaspoon ground chili

Marinate lamb in teriyaki sauce for 1–12 hours.

Heat oil in a frying pan on high. Fry onion and bell pepper for 5 minutes. Add garlic, tomatoes with their liquid, vinegar, maple syrup, pepper and chili. Simmer, uncovered, for 15 minutes or until mixture is slightly thickened.

Preheat a fire in a grill to a high heat. (For wood or charcoal grills, heat to glowing coals. There must be no flames.) Drain meat, reserving marinade to use as a baste. Cook meat, basting occasionally with marinade, for 7–8 minutes on each side, or until sealed, well browned and done to your liking.

SERVES 4

cajun steak

Preheat a fire in a grill to a high heat. (For wood or charcoal barbecues, heat to glowing coals. There must be no flames.)

Brush both sides of steaks with Cajun paste. Cook steaks, basting occasionally with any leftover paste, for about 2–3 minutes each side, or until well browned and sealed. For rare, remove at this stage. For medium or well done, move to a cooler section of the barbecue or reduce to medium heat. Cook, basting steaks occasionally, for a further 2–3 minutes each side for medium, or 4–5 minutes each side for well done.

Serve with mixed salad greens, strips of bell pepper (capsicum) and lemon wedges.

SERVES 4

8 rib-eye or beef fillet steaks, or 4 lamb shoulderblade chops, 3/4 in/2 cm thick

5 oz/155 g prepared Cajun flavoring paste

Lemon wedges, to serve

spinach-stuffed lamb

Prepare a fire in a kettle-type grill. Allow to heat for at least 1 hour with the lid off.

Heat oil for stuffing in a shallow pan and fry onion until tender. Add spinach and cook until soft; drain. Combine onion and spinach with breadcrumbs, almonds, egg and rosemary. Spread over inside of lamb. Roll up and tie with wet string to keep lamb in shape while it cooks. Weigh lamb to calculate cooking time.

Combine marmalade, butter and 1 teaspoon rosemary leaves. Spread mixture over surface of lamb. Cook lamb, covered, with vent open, brushing occasionally with cooking juices. For each 1 lb/500 g, allow 20–25 minutes for rare, 25–30 minutes for medium, or 30–35 minutes for well done. Total cooking time will be about 1 1/4 hours. Remove lamb from grill and leave to rest for 20 minutes in a warm place, covered loosely with foil, before carving.

SERVES 4–6

1 leg of lamb, butterflied

1/4 cup/2 fl oz/60 ml marmalade

1 tablespoon butter, softened

1 teaspoon rosemary leaves

stuffing

1 tablespoon olive oil

1 medium onion, chopped

12 oz/375 g chopped fresh spinach

4 oz/125 g fresh breadcrumbs

1 oz/30 g flaked almonds, toasted

1 egg, lightly beaten

1 teaspoon rosemary leaves

grilled beef tacos

1 1/2 lb/750 g trimmed skirt, flank or tri-tip steaks

Salt and freshly ground black pepper

2 cloves garlic, minced

2 tablespoons olive oil

Juice of 1 lime

18 small or 12 large corn tortillas

garnishes

2 tablespoons coarsely chopped fresh cilantro (fresh coriander/ Chinese parsley) leaves

2 avocados, pitted, peeled and diced

2 tomatoes, seeded and diced

6 green (spring) onions, including the tender green tops, sliced on the diagonal

1/4 head white cabbage, shredded

quick salsa

Process 4 ripe plum (Roma) tomatoes, seeded and coarsely chopped, in a food processor fitted with the metal blade, with 2 fresh serrano chilies, stemmed and coarsely chopped, 1/4 cup/2 fl oz/60 ml fresh lime juice, 1 teaspoon salt and 1/2 teaspoon freshly ground black pepper. Pour into a bowl and set aside.

MAKES ABOUT 1 1/4 CUPS/ 10 FL OZ/310 ML)

 Prepare a fire in a grill. Prepare all the garnishes and place in separate serving bowls.

Ten minutes before grill is ready, season steaks evenly with salt and black pepper, rub with garlic and olive oil, then drizzle evenly with lime juice.

Just before grilling steaks, warm tortillas on the grill: fill a shallow pan with water and, one at a time, briefly dip each tortilla in water and immediately place on the grill rack. Grill for 30 seconds, then turn and grill for 30 seconds longer. Stack tortillas as they come off the grill and wrap them in a damp towel and then in aluminum foil until serving time. (They will keep warm for up to 30 minutes.)

When fire is very hot, place steaks on the grill rack about 3 in/7.5 cm from the coals and grill, turning once, for 1–2 minutes each side, or until evenly caramelized on the outside but still pink in the center.

Transfer steaks to a cutting board and let rest for 3–5 minutes before slicing. Using a sharp knife, cut across the grain into slices about 1/4 in/6 mm thick. Serve immediately with warmed tortillas, quick salsa (*see recipe in box left*) and garnishes. Let diners assemble their own tacos at the table.

SERVES 6

indian raan

 Combine curry paste with yogurt, ground almonds and sugar. Coat lamb shanks with mixture and set aside to marinate for about 1 hour so flavors will develop.

Prepare a fire in a kettle-type grill. Cook shanks, basting frequently with marinade, covered, over indirect heat, following the grill manufacturer's instructions, for 1½–2 hours, or until the meat feels tender when pierced with a fork. Let stand in a warm place for 5 minutes to rest. Serve with naan bread and pickles, if desired.

2 tablespoons prepared rogan josh curry paste, or curry paste of your choice

About 1 cup/8 oz/ 250 g plain yogurt

1 oz/30 g ground almonds

1 oz/30 g brown sugar

8 lamb shanks

Naan bread, to serve

Pickles or chutney, to serve (optional)

SERVES 4

coconut
lamb racks

2 oz/60 g coconut
milk powder

¹/₄ cup/2 fl oz/60 ml
boiling water

2 teaspoons Madras
curry powder

5¹/₂ oz/170 g canned
mango pulp

4 lamb loin racks

1 fresh mango, peeled,
pitted and sliced
(optional)

Prepare a fire in a kettle-type grill. Allow to heat for at least 1 hour with the lid off.

Combine coconut milk powder with boiling water, curry powder and mango pulp. Set 2 tablespoons of the mixture aside to use as a glaze; keep remainder for a sauce.

Place lamb in grill, brush with glaze. Cover and roast, with the vent open, brushing occasionally with glaze, until done to your liking. Allow 30–35 minutes for rare, 35–40 minutes for medium, or 40–45 minutes for well done.

Remove from grill. Leave racks to rest for 10 minutes in a warm place, covered loosely with aluminum foil, before carving.

Serve with the mango sauce, gently warmed, and fresh mango slices (optional).

SERVES 4

curry lamb roast

Prepare a fire in a kettle-type grill. Allow to heat for at least 1 hour with the lid off.

Weigh lamb to calculate cooking time. Brush tandoori paste over entire surface of lamb.

Roast lamb in grill, covered, with the vent open, brushing occasionally with any leftover tandoori paste, until done to your liking. For each 1 lb/500 g, allow 20–25 minutes for rare, 25–30 minutes for medium, or 30–35 minutes for well done. The total cooking time will be about 1 hour. When cooked, remove from grill. Leave to rest for 20 minutes in a warm place, covered loosely with aluminum foil.

Combine yogurt with chopped mint.

Serve lamb with naan bread, warmed briefly in the oven, mustard(s) and yogurt sauce.

SERVES 4

1 leg of lamb or cut of lamb of your choice

5 oz/155 g prepared tandoori curry paste

Naan bread, to serve

Mustard(s) of your choice, to serve

yogurt sauce

8 oz/250 g plain yogurt

2 tablespoons chopped mint

stuffings for roasted meat

If you don't feel confident about cutting a pocket in your roast, have a butcher do it for you. Stuff loosely, because stuffing will expand during cooking. Secure with string or skewers.

bell pepper and leek

Roast 1 medium red bell pepper (capsicum) on a rack in a covered kettle-type grill while grill is heating. Cook until the skin is bubbly and blackened. Place bell pepper in a paper bag and allow to cool. Remove skin from bell pepper and chop flesh.

Cook 1 medium leek, sliced, in microwave oven on High (100% power) for 1 minute.

Combine a quarter of the bell pepper with a quarter of the leek and 1 teaspoon grated fresh ginger root. Use as a stuffing. Serve remaining mixture as an accompaniment.

mango walnut

Thoroughly combine the diced flesh of 1 small mango with 1 oz/30 g fresh breadcrumbs, 1 oz/30 g chopped walnuts and 1 tablespoon apricot jam. (Peaches or apples are also suitable to use when mangoes are unavailable, and pecans or cashews can be substituted for walnuts, if desired.)

kiwifruit

Thoroughly combine 1 tablespoon chopped fresh mint leaves with 2 kiwifruit, peeled and mashed, and 1 oz/30 g soft breadcrumbs made with day-old bread.

tomato and basil

Thoroughly combine 2 oz/60 g seasoned packet stuffing mix with 1 large tomato, chopped and with seeds removed, and 2 teaspoons each finely chopped fresh parsley and basil. Season to taste.

mexican sausages
with chili beans

5 oz/155 g cream cheese, softened

Chili sauce, to taste

8 snow peas (mangetouts)

14 oz/440 g can red kidney beans, drained

1 teaspoon ground cumin

1 ripe tomato, chopped

8 thick beef sausages

2 small carrots, sliced into 8 thin strips

Mix cream cheese with chili sauce in a small bowl. Plunge snow peas briefly into boiling water and refresh under cold, running water.

Prepare a fire in a grill. Heat kidney beans in a saucepan on the grill with cumin, tomato and a little chili sauce (optional).

Grill sausages for 10–15 minutes, turning occasionally. Slit lengthways, but not right through. Fill with cheese mixture, insert a snow pea and carrot strip in each. Serve with chili beans.

SERVES 4

party rolls

1 medium onion, finely chopped

1 small potato, coarsely grated

1 small carrot, grated

1 lb/500 g lean ground (minced) beef

2 tablespoons barbecue sauce

4 oz/125 g cooked rice

1 small egg, beaten

Lavash bread

Cook onion in a microwave oven on High (100% power) for 1 minute. Drain on paper kitchen towels along with grated potato and carrot; the mixture must not be too moist or patties will be soggy.

Combine all ingredients, except lavash bread, in a large bowl. Form the mixture into 24 small, even fingers.

Prepare a fire in a grill to medium heat. Grill fingers on hotplate for 10 minutes, turning occasionally. Serve wrapped in small strips of lavash bread with a dipping sauce of your choice.

SERVES 4–6

cheese-filled
hamburger patties

Combine meat, sauces and onion. Divide mixture into 8 portions and shape evenly into thick, flat patties.

Prepare a fire in a grill to medium heat. Place a cheese slice on 4 of the patties. Drain pineapple, spoon onto patties and top with remaining patties. Carefully mold patty so that it encases cheese completely (no visible joins). Grill, turning occasionally, for 15–20 minutes, or until done to your liking. Assemble in usual way.

SERVES 4

1¼ lb/625 g lean ground (minced) beef

1 tablespoon prepared barbecue sauce

2 tablespoons tomato ketchup (sauce)

1 small onion, finely chopped

4 slices Cheddar, Brie, Camembert or blue-vein cheese

7 oz/220 g can crushed pineapple

chicken and pork

Always watch chicken and pork carefully on the grill so that they don't overcook and dry out. To test chicken for doneness, pierce the thickest part of the meat with a skewer—the juices that run out should be clear. Many people prefer pork to be well done, but it's really a matter of personal preference.

firecracker
chicken thighs

1¹/₂–2 lb/750 g–1 kg chicken thighs

2–3 tablespoons hot bean paste

2 tablespoons soy sauce

2 tablespoons sesame seeds, toasted
in a 350°F/180°C/Gas Mark 4 oven
for 7–10 minutes and crushed

1 tablespoon sesame oil

1 tablespoon sugar

1 oz/30 g finely chopped green
(spring) onions

4 large cloves garlic, minced

¹/₄ teaspoon salt

¹/₈ teaspoon pepper

Remove skin from chicken thighs. Score meat on both sides with shallow diagonal cuts about 1 in/2.5 cm apart.

Combine bean paste, soy sauce, sesame seeds, sesame oil, sugar, green onion, garlic, salt and pepper in a large mixing bowl; stir well. Pour into a plastic bag; add chicken thighs. Seal bag and turn to coat chicken. Marinate in refrigerator for 4–24 hours, turning bag occasionally. Remove chicken, scraping off excess marinade. Reserve marinade.

Prepare a fire in a grill. Place chicken on the grill rack. Grill directly over medium coals for 15 minutes. Turn chicken over and grill for 10–15 minutes more. Baste both sides with reserved marinade and grill, turning once, for 5 minutes more, or until chicken is tender and no pink remains. Discard any remaining marinade.

Serve with grilled vegetables or a salad of your choice.

SERVES 4

two spicy
marinades

ONE Combine 2 tablespoons good-quality olive oil with 2 tablespoons dry Italian white wine in a large non-aluminum dish. Stir in 6 large cloves garlic, minced, 4–6 teaspoons fresh oregano leaves or 2–3 teaspoons dried oregano and red pepper flakes (cayenne pepper) to taste (small fresh or dried chilies can be used instead, if liked).

two Combine 2¹/₂ cups/20 fl oz/625 ml dry red wine with 2 cups/16 fl oz/500 ml good-quality olive oil, ¹/₂ cup/4 fl oz/125 ml port, ¹/₄ cup/2 fl oz/60 ml each balsamic vinegar and Dijon mustard in a large non-aluminum dish. Stir in 2 large cloves garlic, minced, 2 onions, sliced, 2 bay leaves, crumbled, a few sprigs parsley, 2 tablespoons brown sugar and 1 teaspoon black pepper-corns. Stir until well combined.

chicken satay

2 lb/1 kg boneless, skinless chicken breasts, thinly sliced

1 tablespoon vegetable oil

Fresh cilantro (fresh coriander/Chinese parsley) sprigs, for garnish

satay sauce

1 cup/4 oz/125 g roasted unsalted peanuts

1 tablespoon vegetable oil

1 onion, finely chopped

2 cloves garlic, minced

2 teaspoons chopped fresh chilies

1 tablespoon chopped fresh lemongrass—if lemongrass is not available, substitute 2 teaspoons grated lemon or lime zest (rind)

2 teaspoons curry powder

1 teaspoon ground cumin

$1^1/_2$ cups/12 fl oz/375 ml unsweetened coconut milk

2 tablespoons packed brown sugar

2 teaspoons lime juice

Soak 12 bamboo skewers in water for at least 30 minutes to prevent scorching.

Blend or process peanuts for satay sauce until crushed. Heat oil in a frying pan, add onion, garlic, chili, lemongrass, curry powder and cumin, and cook, stirring, until onion is soft. Add nuts and remaining ingredients and stir until hot.

Prepare a fire in a grill. Thread chicken onto skewers and brush with oil. Grill skewers for about 10 minutes, or until tender.

Serve skewers on a bed of thinly sliced vegetables, if desired, with satay sauce spooned over.

SERVES 6

butterflying whole chicken

◀ one

Removing Backbone Set the bird, breast-side-down, on the cutting board. With poultry shears or a sharp knife, cut closely along one side of the backbone, then the other; discard the backbone.

butterflied
citrus chicken

 Using poultry shears or a sharp knife, cut closely along both sides of backbone for the entire length of the chicken. Discard backbone. Open bird out as flat as possible, skin-side-up. Cover with clear plastic wrap (film). Strike breast firmly in the center with the flat side of a meat mallet. (This breaks the breastbone so bird lies flat.) Twist wing tips under the back. Halfway between legs and breastbone, near the tip of the breast, cut a 1-in/2.5-cm slit through the skin on either side of and parallel with the breastbone. Insert drumstick tips into the slits.

Combine olive oil, orange juice, lemon juice, rosemary, garlic, salt and pepper in a small mixing bowl; stir well. Pour into a large plastic bag; add chicken. Seal bag and turn to coat chicken with marinade. Place bag in a large baking dish and marinate chicken in the refrigerator for 8 to 24 hours, turning bag occasionally. Drain marinade from chicken, reserving marinade.

Arrange medium-hot coals around a drip pan in a kettle-type grill, then test for medium heat above the pan. Place chicken, skin-side-up, on grill rack directly over the drip pan, not over the coals. Brush with some of the reserved marinade. Cover and cook for 30 minutes. Brush with additional marinade. Cook for 30–40 minutes more, or until chicken is tender and no pink remains. Discard remaining marinade.

SERVES 4

1 whole broiler-fryer (roasting) chicken, about 2¹/₂–3 lb/1.25–1.5 kg

¹/₃ cup/2¹/₂ fl oz/80 ml olive oil or cooking oil

¹/₃ cup/2¹/₂ fl oz/80 ml orange juice

¹/₄ cup/2 fl oz/60 ml lemon juice

1¹/₂ teaspoons dried rosemary, crushed

2 cloves garlic, minced

¹/₂ teaspoon salt

¹/₄ teaspoon pepper

◀ two

Flattening Bird Turn the chicken skin-side-up with breast farthest from you, wings up, legs down. Open the bird as flat as possible. Cover its surface with a large sheet of plastic wrap (film). Flatten by striking the breast firmly in the center with the smooth side of a meat mallet to break the breastbone.

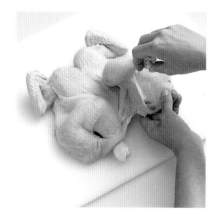

◀ three

Tucking Legs into Slits Cut a 1-in/2.5-cm slit through the loose skin on either side of and parallel with the breastbone halfway between legs and breastbone, near bottom tip of breast. Insert tips of drumsticks into slits to secure them so the bird remains flat during the grilling process.

grilled citrus-flavored
chicken breast

1 cup/8 fl oz/250 ml fresh
orange juice

2 tablespoons fresh
lime juice

1 dried chipotle chili,
stemmed and seeded

1 cup/8 fl oz/250 ml red
salsa (*see recipe in
box below center*)

¹/4 cup/2 fl oz/60 ml
olive oil

1 teaspoon salt

4 chicken breast fillets

Fresh orange slices
(optional)

Fresh cilantro (fresh
coriander/Chinese parsley)
sprigs (optional)

Combine orange juice, lime juice and chili in a small saucepan and bring to the boil. Reduce heat to medium and simmer, uncovered, for about 5 minutes, or until chili is plump. Remove from heat and let cool.

Transfer cooled citrus mixture to a blender and add salsa (*recipe below*), olive oil and salt. Purée until smooth.

Rinse chicken fillets and pat dry. Place in a shallow non-aluminum dish. Pour

purée evenly over top, cover and let marinate in the refrigerator for 2–4 hours.

Prepare a fire in a grill. When hot, remove chicken fillets from marinade. Place, skin-side-down, on grill rack about 5 in/13 cm from the coals and grill for 2–3 minutes. Turn and cook on the second side for 2–3 minutes. Continue to cook fillets, turning every 2–3 minutes to avoid burning, until tender and opaque throughout. Total cooking time should be about 12–20 minutes, depending upon size of breasts.

Transfer fillets to a warmed platter. Garnish with orange slices and cilantro sprigs, if desired, and serve immediately.

SERVES 4

red salsa

Warm 2 tablespoons vegetable oil in a saucepan over medium heat. Add 1 yellow onion, thinly sliced, and cook for about 10 minutes, or until softened. Add 2 cloves garlic, sliced, 1 fresh jalapeño chili, stemmed, seeded and thinly sliced, and 1 teaspoon salt, or to taste. Cook for 2 minutes more. Add 12 oz/375 g canned plum (Roma) tomatoes with their juice and continue to cook, stirring occasionally, over low heat for 10–15 minutes, or until the tomatoes are soft and the liquid has been reduced to about half the quantity.

japanese
chicken kabobs

Soak 12 bamboo skewers, each about 6 in/15 cm long, in water for 30 minutes to prevent scorching. Combine orange zest, orange juice, sherry, soy sauce, sugar, garlic and ginger in a small mixing bowl. Set aside ¼ cup/ 2 fl oz/60 ml of the marinade mixture to serve with cooked kabobs.

Cut fillets into 1-in/2.5-cm pieces. Cut green onions into 1½-in/4-cm lengths. Thread 3 chicken pieces and 2 onion pieces onto each wooden skewer, alternating chicken and onions. Place kabobs in a shallow dish and pour marinade over. Marinate at room temperature for 30 minutes, turning once. Remove kabobs from marinade, reserving marinade.

Prepare a fire in a grill. When hot, grill kabobs on the rack for 8–10 minutes, or until chicken is tender and no pink remains. Turn and brush with used reserved marinade once during cooking.

Meanwhile, boil unused reserved marinade for several minutes. Serve with kabobs, rice and pickled ginger, if desired.

SERVES 4

1 teaspoon finely shredded orange zest (rind)

½ cup/4 fl oz/125 ml orange juice

⅓ cup/2½ fl oz/80 ml dry sherry

¼ cup/2 fl oz/60 ml soy sauce

2 teaspoons sugar

1 clove garlic, minced

½ teaspoon grated ginger root

12 oz/375 g skinless chicken breast fillets

6 to 8 green (spring) onions

Hot cooked rice

Pickled ginger (optional)

Let cool slightly. Transfer to a blender or food processor and purée until smooth. Strain through a sieve placed over a bowl. Set aside to cool completely for use as a table salsa, or reheat gently to use hot. Will keep for up to 4 days if covered tightly and stored in the refrigerator, or for up to 1 month in the freezer.

MAKES ABOUT
2 CUPS/16 FL OZ/500 ML

blackened chicken
with tomato-chili sauce

6 skinless, single chicken breast fillets

1 tablespoon plus 1 teaspoon paprika

2 teaspoons black pepper

1/2 teaspoon red pepper flakes
(cayenne pepper), or to taste

2 teaspoons garlic powder

2 teaspoons onion powder

1 teaspoon salt

1 teaspoon dried thyme

4 oz/125 g butter, melted

tomato-chili sauce

1/3 cup/21/2 fl oz/80 ml tomato
sauce (purée)

1 tomato, finely chopped

1 tablespoon plus 1 teaspoon
lime juice

1 tablespoon plus 1 teaspoon
chili sauce

1/4 teaspoon Tabasco sauce

1/2 teaspoon salt

2 teaspoons chopped fresh dill

Pepper to taste

make ahead

The spice mix can be made
several weeks ahead. Store in
an airtight jar at room
temperature. The sauce can be
made a day ahead.

Combine all Tomato-Chili Sauce ingredients in a bowl;
mix well. Stand for at least 1 hour.

Pound chicken fillets lightly until of an even thickness.

Combine dry ingredients in a screw-top jar, using more
red pepper flakes if a hotter mix is preferred, and shake well.

Prepare a fire in a grill until very hot. Dip chicken into melted butter
and sprinkle spice mixture on both sides. Cook chicken for about
2 minutes on each side, or until a black crust forms and the chicken
is cooked through. (This cooking process will create a lot of smoke and
is best done outdoors. If cooking indoors, use a cast-iron skillet or
a broiler pan and have a strong exhaust fan operating.)

Serve chicken with Tomato-Chili Sauce and some extra melted butter,
if desired.

SERVES 6

grilled
chicken kabobs

For marinade, combine onion with garlic, lemon juice, paprika, red pepper flakes, $1/2$ teaspoon black pepper and the thyme in a blender or a food processor fitted with a metal blade. Use rapid on-off pulses to combine well. Add yogurt and pulse to mix.

Rinse chicken and pat dry. Cut into 1-in/2.5-cm cubes and place in a non-aluminum container. Pour yogurt mixture over chicken and turn to coat. Cover and let marinate in refrigerator for 8 hours.

Prepare a fire in a grill. Remove chicken pieces from marinade, reserving marinade, and thread onto metal skewers. Brush chicken with olive oil and sprinkle with salt and pepper.

Place skewers on an oiled grill rack and grill, turning and basting once with reserved marinade for 4–5 minutes each side for breast meat and 5–6 minutes each side for thigh meat, or until no longer pink in the center when cut into with a knife.

Transfer skewers to warmed individual plates or a platter. Serve hot.

SERVES 4

$1^1/2$ lb/750 g boneless, skinless chicken breasts or thighs

Olive oil, for brushing

Salt

marinade

1 large yellow onion, chopped

4 cloves garlic, minced

$1/4$ cup/2 fl oz/60 ml fresh lemon juice

1 tablespoon paprika

$1/2$ teaspoon ground red pepper flakes (cayenne pepper)

$1/2$ teaspoon freshly ground black pepper, plus pepper to taste

1 tablespoon chopped fresh thyme

1 cup/8 oz/250 g plain yogurt

vegetable kabobs

If you like, thread vegetable pieces of similar size on separate skewers, brush with olive oil or flavored oil, such as rosemary or garlic oil, and place on grill when meat is nearly cooked. Remove kabobs when vegetables are done to your liking and serve with pita bread or pilaf.

bacon-wrapped
chicken drumsticks
with plum sauce

8 chicken drumsticks

1/2 teaspoon salt

1/2 teaspoon pepper

1 small garlic clove
(optional), minced

8 rashers bacon

1 tablespoon vegetable oil

plum sauce

4 oz/125 g plum jam

1 tablespoon apple cider vinegar,
or to taste

1 tablespoon mild chili sauce,
or to taste

 Prepare a fire in a grill. Rub drumsticks with salt, pepper and garlic, if using. Wrap a strip of bacon firmly around each drumstick, securing ends with toothpicks. Brush with vegetable oil and grill, turning frequently and brushing with additional oil, for about 12 minutes, or until cooked through. To test for doneness, pierce meat in the thickest part with a thin skewer. The juices that run out should be clear.

Heat jam for sauce with apple cider vinegar and chili sauce in a small pan or microwave oven and beat together. Arrange hot drumsticks on a platter around a dish of the sauce for dipping.

SERVES 4

make ahead

Drumsticks can be prepared ahead to the point where they are ready to cook, wrapped in plastic wrap (film) and frozen or refrigerated until needed. Sauce can be made several days in advance and refrigerated. Defrost frozen chicken overnight in the refrigerator.

grilled squab
with garlic and ginger

Rinse and dry squab thoroughly; cut in half down the backbone and press out flat. Rub with a little oil. Mix ginger, garlic, 3/4 teaspoon salt and pepper together and rub evenly over squab. Set aside for at least 1 hour.

Prepare a fire in a grill. Cook squab, brushing occasionally with remaining oil. Turn several times and cook until surface is golden-brown and meat feels firm when pressed. Place vegetables in a dish. Mix remaining salt with sugar and vinegar and pour over vegetables. Knead with the fingers for a few minutes until softened. Arrange squab on warmed plates and garnish with vinegared vegetables.

SERVES 4

4 squab

3 tablespoons vegetable oil

1 tablespoon finely grated ginger root

2 large garlic cloves, minced

1 1/2 teaspoons salt

1/2 teaspoon black pepper

1 medium onion, thinly sliced

1 small cucumber, thinly sliced

1 medium carrot, thinly sliced

2 teaspoons sugar

1 1/2 tablespoons white wine vinegar

marinate ahead

Vegetables can be marinated for up to 2 days ahead; store in a covered container in the refrigerator. Marinate squab for up to 1 day ahead; store in the refrigerator, covered tightly with plastic wrap (film).

grilled
five-spice chicken

2 small chickens,
about 2 lb/1 kg each

marinade

1 piece ginger root, 1 in/2.5 cm long,
peeled and grated

4 cloves garlic, chopped

2 shallots, chopped

1 1/2 tablespoons brown sugar

1/2 teaspoon salt

1/4 teaspoon freshly ground pepper

1/2 teaspoon five-spice powder

2 tablespoons Vietnamese
or Thai fish sauce

2 tablespoons soy sauce

1 tablespoon dry sherry

Cut each chicken in half through breast and backbone. Using your palms, press down on breast to flatten the halves out slightly.

Process combined ginger, garlic, shallots, brown sugar and salt to a smooth paste in a blender or mini food processor, or with a mortar and pestle. Transfer marinade to a large, shallow, non-aluminum bowl. Add pepper, five-spice powder, fish sauce, soy sauce and sherry and stir to mix well. Add chicken halves and turn to coat thoroughly with marinade. Cover and marinate in the refrigerator for 4–12 hours.

Prepare a fire in a charcoal grill. When coals are ash white, place chicken halves, bone-side-down, on the grill rack about 4 in/10 cm above coals and grill for 20 minutes. Turn chicken over and continue to grill for about 20 minutes longer, or until thoroughly cooked and golden brown with nice grill marks. Serve hot with dipping sauce (*see recipe in box below*).

SERVES 4

dipping sauce

Using a mortar and pestle, mash 1 clove garlic, finely minced, 1 small, fresh red chili, seeded and finely minced, and 1/4 cup/2 oz/60 g sugar to a paste. Add 1/4 cup/2 fl oz/60 ml fresh lime juice, including pulp, 3 fl oz/100 ml Vietnamese or Thai fish sauce and 1/2 cup/4 fl oz/125 ml water and stir to dissolve sugar. Strain sauce into a bowl or jar and use immediately. Or sauce can be stored, refrigerated and tightly covered, for up to 5 days.

spicy
spanish kabobs

1/4 cup/2 fl oz/60 ml olive oil
or cooking oil

1 tablespoon lemon juice

2 tablespoons snipped
fresh parsley

1/2 teaspoon ground cumin

1/4–1/2 teaspoon crushed red
pepper flakes (cayenne pepper)

1/2 teaspoon dried thyme,
crushed

1/2 teaspoon paprika

1/8 teaspoon saffron threads,
crushed

1/4 teaspoon salt

1/4 teaspoon black pepper

12 oz/375 g boneless, skinless
chicken thighs, cut into
1-in/2.5-cm cubes, or strips
1 in/2.5 cm wide and
2 in/5 cm long

 Combine oil, lemon juice, parsley, cumin, red pepper flakes, thyme, paprika, saffron, salt and black pepper in a medium mixing bowl; stir well. Pour into a plastic bag; add chicken pieces. Seal bag; turn to coat chicken with marinade. Marinate in refrigerator for 4–24 hours, turning bag occasionally. Drain marinade from chicken, reserving marinade.

Thread chicken pieces on 4 long metal skewers, leaving about 1/4 in/6 mm between pieces. Prepare a fire in a grill. Place chicken kabobs on grill rack and cook over medium coals, turning once and brushing occasionally with reserved marinade, for 10–12 minutes, or until chicken is tender and no pink remains.

Serve on a bed of saffron rice.

SERVES 4

cornish game hens
with vegetables and aïoli

2 Cornish game hens or baby chickens, about 1³/₄ lb/875 g each

¹/₂ cup/4 fl oz/125 ml olive oil

¹/₄ cup/2 fl oz/60 ml lemon juice

2 cloves garlic, minced

4 green (spring) onions, chopped

1 tablespoon chopped fresh thyme

4 thin Oriental (ladyfinger) eggplant (aubergines)

2 zucchini (courgettes)

2 yellow squash zucchini (courgettes)

2 red bell peppers (capsicums)

4 medium red-skinned potatoes

Coarse salt

Freshly ground black pepper

aïoli

Blend or process 2 egg yolks, ¹/₄ teaspoon salt and 2 cloves garlic, peeled and minced, until smooth. With motor running, gradually add ²/₃ cup/5 fl oz/160 ml vegetable oil and ¹/₃ cup/2¹/₂ fl oz/80 ml olive oil in a thin, steady stream until the mixture is thick. Transfer to a bowl and stir in 1 tablespoon fresh lemon juice.

Using poultry shears or a sharp knife, cut along either side of backbones of birds (*see pages 44–5*). Remove and discard backbones. Place each bird, breast-side-up, on a work surface and flatten with your hand. Combine oil, lemon juice, garlic, green onions and thyme and brush chickens with some of this mixture.

Prepare a fire in a kettle-type grill. Cook chickens over very low heat, turning once during cooking, for about 30 minutes, or until almost tender. (If your grill doesn't have a cover for slow cooking, bake chickens at 375°F/190°C/Gas Mark 4 for about 30 minutes, or until almost tender, and finish cooking on a grill to brown and produce a smoky flavor.)

Thinly slice eggplants and zucchini lengthways. Cut bell peppers into thick strips, discarding ribs and seeds; thinly slice potatoes. Brush vegetables with some of the oil mixture and grill beside chickens for about 10 minutes, or until well browned and tender. Drizzle with remaining oil mixture and serve with salt, pepper and aïoli (*recipe in box left*).

SERVES 4 TO 6

chicken breasts
with tomato-mint pesto

2–3 tablespoons packed fresh
mint leaves

2–3 tablespoons packed fresh parsley
sprigs, with stems removed

1 oz/30 g dried tomatoes

¼ cup/2 fl oz/60 ml olive oil

1 clove garlic, halved

1½ teaspoons finely shredded
lemon zest (rind)

¼ teaspoon salt

⅛ teaspoon lemon-pepper seasoning

4 medium chicken breast halves,
about 1 lb/500g total

Process mint leaves, parsley, dried tomatoes, olive oil, garlic, lemon zest, salt and lemon-pepper seasoning in a blender container or food processor bowl until finely chopped. Set pesto aside.

Remove skin from chicken, if desired. Cut a pocket in each chicken fillet by cutting a 2-in/5-cm-deep slit on the breastbone side of the fillet. Fill each pocket with a fourth of the pesto.

Prepare a fire in a grill. Place breasts, skin-side-down, on grill rack and grill 4–5 in/10–13 cm from the heat for 20 minutes. Turn chicken and cook for 5–15 minutes more, or until meat is tender and no pink remains. Juices that run when meat is pierced should be clear. Serve with a simple rice pilaf or a green salad.

SERVES 4

making chicken pockets

◀ one

Cutting Pockets Place each chicken breast fillet on a cutting board, skin-side-up. With a small knife or boning knife, make a pocket 2 in/5 cm deep and about 3 in/7.5 cm long in breastbone side of the meat.

◀ two

Filling Pockets Combine all pesto filling ingredients in a food processor or blender. Hold open pocket of one breast fillet and spoon in a fourth of the pesto mixture. Repeat with remaining breast fillets and filling.

marinated honeyed
pork spareribs

1 cup/8 fl oz/250 ml
plum sauce

1 cup/8 fl oz/250 ml
barbecue sauce

1 cup/8 fl oz/250 ml
sweet sherry

1 cup/8 fl oz/250 ml
olive oil or safflower oil

1/2 cup/4 fl oz/125 ml
honey

1 teaspoon ground cumin

1 teaspoon ground
cardamom

1 teaspoon ground
turmeric

4 lb/2 kg pork spareribs

Combine all ingredients, except ribs, in a large shallow dish. Add ribs and baste with marinade. Allow to marinate in refrigerator for about 12 hours, brushing frequently with marinade. Prepare a fire in a grill. Grill ribs, basting frequently with marinade and turning during cooking, for about 40 minutes, or until done to your liking.

Serve with corn on the cob with sweet butter (*recipe in box right*) or grilled vegetables or salads of your choice.

SERVES 8

corn on the cob
with sweet butter

Process 8 oz/250 g softened butter in a food processor with 2 tablespoons grated orange zest (rind) and 1/4 teaspoon each of ground cardamom, ground cinnamon and ground nutmeg until combined. Refrigerate until ready to use.

Remove and reserve dark green outer husks from 8 cobs of corn. Peel away paler inner husks, leaving them attached at base of cobs. Remove silk, replace husks over corn kernels and tie with reserved leaves. Soak cobs in water for 30 minutes. Place on grill for about 30 minutes, turning frequently and brushing with oil. Serve corn with butter.

glazed ham
and mango parcels

Oil or melted butter, for brushing

4 thick ham steaks

1¹/₂ tablespoons brown sugar

1 oz/30 g butter, softened

Salt and black pepper

2 fresh medium-size mangoes

Cut 4 pieces of aluminum foil, each 12 in/30 cm square. Brush with oil or melted butter. Place a steak on each sheet. Make a paste with brown sugar, butter, salt and pepper and spread thickly over one side of each steak. Peel and thickly slice mangoes and spread slices evenly over each steak, using ¹/₂ mango for each. Wrap foil around parcels, and fold edges together to seal.

Prepare a fire in a grill. Grill parcels for about 6 minutes. (Can also be baked on a baking sheet in a moderate oven/375°F/190°C/Gas Mark 4 for 15 minutes.)

SERVES 4

honey-glazed
drumsticks

Combine honey, soy sauce, vinegar and, if desired, molasses in a small saucepan. Cook over medium-low heat, stirring occasionally, for about 5 minutes, or until bubbly. (Watch mixture closely, as it will foam.)

Meanwhile, prepare a fire in a grill. Remove skin from drumsticks, if desired; rinse drumsticks and pat dry. Place on a rack and grill 5–6 in/13–15 cm from heat for about 15 minutes, or until chicken is light brown. Turn chicken and grill for 10–15 minutes more, or until chicken is tender and no pink remains. Brush with glaze in the last 5–10 minutes of cooking. Before serving, spoon remaining glaze over drumsticks.

¹/₄ cup/2 fl oz/ 60 ml honey

2 tablespoons soy sauce

1 tablespoon apple cider vinegar

1 tablespoon molasses (optional)

8 chicken drumsticks, about 2¹/₄ lb/1.125 kg total

SERVES 4

pork chops
with chutney

Trim excess fat from pork chops; season chops with salt and pepper. Make a paste with chutney and vindaloo and brush over both sides of each chop. Set remainder aside.

Prepare a fire in a grill. Grill chops over moderately hot coals, brushing with oil and turning frequently. When almost done, thickly spread remaining chutney over one side and continue to cook on other side until done. Serve with white rice and a cucumber salad.

SERVES 4

4 large pork chops

1/2 teaspoon salt

1/3 teaspoon black pepper

3 tablespoons fruit chutney

1 teaspoon vindaloo paste, or other hot curry sauce

2-3 tablespoons vegetable oil

pork satay

2 tablespoons brown sugar

1 teaspoon ground cumin

1½ teaspoons ground coriander

½ teaspoon ground turmeric

1 tablespoon fresh lime juice

1½ teaspoons Thai fish sauce

2 tablespoons coconut cream

1½ lb/750 g pork butt or tenderloin, cut into ¾-in/2-cm cubes

satay sauce

1 oz/30 g tamarind pulp, coarsely chopped

½ cup/4 fl oz/125 ml boiling water

1 tablespoon peanut or corn oil

2 tablespoons prepared red curry paste

1 tablespoon sweet paprika

1 cup/8 fl oz/250 ml coconut milk

1½ oz/45 g ground dry-roasted peanuts or 3 oz/90 g chunky peanut butter

2 tablespoons palm sugar or brown sugar

1 tablespoon fish sauce

½ teaspoon salt

 Combine brown sugar with cumin, coriander, turmeric, lime juice, fish sauce and coconut cream in a bowl; stir well. Add pork and mix well to coat. Marinate, covered, for 2 hours at room temperature. Soak 18 bamboo skewers, each 8 in/20 cm long, in water for at least 30 minutes.

Soak tamarind pulp in the boiling water in a small bowl for 15 minutes. Mash with the back of a fork to help disperse the pulp. Pour through a fine-mesh sieve into another small bowl, pressing against the pulp to extract as much liquid as possible. Discard pulp; set the liquid aside.

Heat oil in a wok or saucepan over medium heat. Add curry paste and paprika, reduce heat to low and cook, stirring, for 1 minute. Add coconut milk and stir continuously over low heat for about 3 minutes, or until red-stained oil weeps from the paste. Add ground peanuts and palm sugar and simmer, stirring occasionally, for about 5 minutes. Stir in tamarind liquid, fish sauce and salt and cook for 1 minute longer. If sauce is too thick, thin with a little water. Remove from heat and keep warm.

Prepare a fire in a grill or preheat a gas grill to medium-high heat. Thread 4 or 5 pieces of pork onto each skewer. Pieces should touch but do not press them together. Place skewers on grill rack and grill for about 2 minutes, or until there are grill marks on the underside. Turn skewers over and continue grilling for about 1 minute longer, or until pork is browned on all sides and firm to the touch. Transfer skewers to a platter. Serve sauce in a shallow bowl alongside with rice and/or vegetables.

SERVES 6

grilled vegetables

What could be easier or more delicious than grilled vegetables? Serve with any type of grilled meat along with fresh salads and good bread.

butternut squash

Halve squash lengthwise. Remove seeds but do not peel. Partly cook in microwave oven on High (100% power) for 8–10 minutes. Place on rack in a covered grill and cook for about 30 minutes, or until tender.

cheesy potatoes in their jackets

Scrub medium-size potatoes clean. Prick skins well all over. Place in a paper bag and partly cook in a microwave oven on High (100% power), allowing 2 minutes for each potato (cook in batches if you are doing a lot). Make slashes in potatoes with a sharp knife. Push grated cheese, such as Cheddar or Gruyère, and chopped fresh herbs, such as thyme or marjoram, into the slashes. Wrap each in foil (shiny side in). Place on a rack in a kettle-type grill. Cook for about 30 minutes, or until tender.

vegetable parcels

Prepare vegetables, such as broccoli or cauliflower florets, squares or strips of red and green bell peppers (capsicums), and diagonally sliced carrots and celery. Spray or brush squares of foil with oil and place prepared vegetables in center. Add a sprig of rosemary, if desired. Pull up corners and twist to form domes over vegetables, but leave a vent so that steam can escape. Place on a rack in a covered grill and cook for about 12–15 minutes, or until vegetables are done to your liking.

fish and seafood

Choose fish with firm flesh and good flavor for cooking on the grill. Large deep-sea varieties are easy to handle, either cut into thick steaks or served whole as a spectacular centerpiece for a seafood feast. Crustaceans and shellfish add a flamboyant touch to a barbecue.

marinated whole trout
with olives and chili

8 small trout, cleaned

marinade

½ cup/4 fl oz/125 ml olive oil

¾ cup/6 fl oz/185 ml coconut milk

¼ cup/2 fl oz/60 ml lime juice

2 hot red chilies, chopped

3 oz/90 g stuffed olives

1 onion, chopped

2–3 tablespoons chopped mint leaves

2 limes, sliced

Combine oil, coconut milk, lime juice, chilies, olives, onion and mint in a shallow dish; add lime slices and trout. Refrigerate for at least 4 hours.

Prepare a fire in a grill. When ready to cook, wrap each fish in foil with about 2 tablespoons of marinade and a slice of lime in each parcel. Grill fish for about 8 minutes on each side, or until fish is cooked through. To serve, arrange fish on serving platter and pour on hot marinade.

SERVES 8

marinades

Seafood quickly picks up subtle flavors from an interesting marinade. Pour over seafood and refrigerate for 3–4 hours before cooking. Baste with drained marinade during cooking or include with fish if you are cooking it wrapped in aluminum foil or banana leaves.

one Combine 2 large cloves garlic, minced, with ½ cup/4 fl oz/125 ml each of olive oil and balsamic vinegar in a bowl. Add 1 tablespoon brown sugar and a few sprigs of fresh dill, chopped.

two Dissolve 3 oz/90 g palm sugar in 1 cup/8 fl oz/250 ml coconut cream in a small pan over low heat. Remove from the heat and stir in 1 tablespoon grated lime zest (rind), 2 tablespoons lime juice and 1 or 2 bird's eye chilis, finely chopped.

three Combine 1 cup/8 fl oz/250 ml olive oil with 3 bird's eye chilies, chopped, 1 tablespoon grated ginger root and 1 stalk of lemongrass, pounded.

four Combine ½ cup/4 fl oz/125 ml each of olive oil and lemon juice with 1 clove garlic, minced, and 2 teaspoons capers.

grilled lobster
with spicy butter

Prepare a fire in a grill. Using a sharp knife, pierce lobsters between the eyes to kill them. Working with 1 lobster at a time, place back-side-up on a cutting board and, starting where tail and head sections meet, cut in half lengthways, first cutting the tail portion and then the head. Pull out and discard the intestinal vein and any organs. Season lobster meat to taste with salt and black pepper. Repeat with the remaining lobsters.

Heat the olive oil in a wide sauté pan over medium heat. Add shallots and cook for 3–5 minutes, or until lightly golden. Add garlic and chilies and continue to cook for 1–2 minutes longer. Add cumin, paprika and red pepper flakes and cook, stirring, for 1–2 minutes, or until aromas are released but spices are not burned. Remove from the heat and stir in lime juice, butter, 1 teaspoon salt and 1 teaspoon black pepper.

Place lobsters on the grill rack, shell-side-down, 3–5 in/7.5–13 cm from the coals. Grill, rotating lobster halves onto their sides and moving them away from the hottest part of the fire as necessary to prevent burning, for about 8 minutes, or until meat is opaque. (Do not at any time turn the meat directly toward the fire.)

Spoon butter mixture over lobsters during the last few minutes of grilling. Serve hot with plenty of lime wedges.

SERVES 4

4 live lobsters, 1 1/2 lb/750 g each

Sea salt

Freshly ground black pepper

1/4 cup/2 fl oz/60 ml olive oil

6 shallots, chopped

2 cloves garlic, minced

3 fresh red jalapeño chilies, stemmed, seeded and chopped

3 fresh green jalapeño chilies, stemmed, seeded and chopped

2 teaspoons ground cumin

2 teaspoons paprika

1/2 teaspoon red pepper flakes (cayenne pepper)

Juice of 2 limes

2–3 oz/60–90 g unsalted butter

Lime wedges, to serve

spicy snapper
with dill

Clean fish and make several diagonal slashes on each side. Season inside and out with salt and pepper. On a piece of aluminum foil large enough to enclose fish, spread or brush butter over an area the same size as the fish and place fish on it. Place several lemon slices and a sprig or two of dill in the cavity of the fish and arrange remaining lemon and herbs over fish. Wrap foil around fish, folding edges over to seal.

Prepare a fire in a grill. Cook fish over moderate heat for about 25 minutes for 1 large fish or 15 minutes for 2 smaller fish, or until tender. Test during cooking by inserting a skewer into the thickest part of the fish. If the flesh is tender and white, the fish is done.

SERVES 4

1 or 2 snapper or bream
(about 2 lb/1 kg total weight)

Salt and black pepper

1 oz/30 g butter, or
1 fl oz/30 ml olive or
vegetable oil

1 lemon, sliced

3-4 fresh dill sprigs

fresh sardines
with hot garlic dressing

About 20 minutes before cooking, sprinkle sardines with salt. Prepare a fire in a grill. Brush sardines lightly with oil and cook on a hot grill until just done.

Heat remaining oil in a small pan; add garlic and cook briefly. Pour hot garlic oil over fish and serve at once, garnished with herbs and lemon slices.

SERVES 4

12 fresh sardines

1 1/2 teaspoons coarse salt

1/4 cup/2 fl oz/60 ml olive oil
or vegetable oil

3-4 garlic cloves,
finely chopped

Fresh herbs

Lemon slices, to serve

fish in blankets

marinade

¹/₄ cup/2 fl oz/60 ml olive oil

2 tablespoons chopped fresh
flat-leaf (Italian) parsley
or fennel fronds

2 teaspoons chopped fresh thyme
or dried oregano

Juice of 1 lemon

Salt and freshly ground pepper

2 lb/1 kg large, fresh sardines,
cleaned, with heads left on,
or 4 fish fillets such as sea bass, cod
or sole, about 6 oz/185 g each

Bottled grape leaves, rinsed of brine
and stems removed

Lemon wedges, to serve

dressing

As a change, serve fish with
this simple dressing in place
of the lemon wedges. Whisk
5 tablespoons olive oil with
2–3 tablespoons fresh lemon
juice and a complementary
herb of your choice, chopped.

Whisk olive oil with parsley, thyme and lemon juice in a large, shallow, non-aluminum dish; season with salt and pepper to taste. Add fish and turn to coat well. Let marinate at room temperature for about 1 hour.

Prepare a fire in a grill. Wrap 1 or 2 grape leaves around the center of each whole fish or fillet, leaving head and tail or both ends of each fillet exposed; secure the leaves with toothpicks, if needed.

Place fish packets on an oiled grill rack and grill, turning once, for 7–10 minutes per side for whole fish and 5–6 minutes per side for fish fillets, or until flesh is opaque throughout.

Transfer to a warmed platter and serve hot with lemon wedges.

SERVES 4

grilled
swordfish kabobs

Whisk olive oil with lemon juice, paprika and crushed bay leaves in a shallow, non-aluminum bowl. Add swordfish cubes, turning to coat well. Cover and let marinate in the refrigerator for about 4 hours.

Prepare a fire in a grill. Remove fish cubes from marinade, reserving marinade. Thread cubes onto metal skewers, alternating them with whole bay leaves, lemon slices, bell pepper pieces and cherry tomatoes. Sprinkle with salt and pepper.

Place skewers on an oiled grill rack and grill, turning as needed and basting a few times with the reserved marinade, for about 10 minutes, or until fish is opaque throughout.

Transfer skewers to a warmed platter; serve hot with lemon wedges and plain steamed rice or a simple rice pilaf.

SERVES 4

marinade

1/2 cup/4 fl oz/125 ml olive oil

1/3 cup/2 1/2 fl oz/80 ml fresh lemon juice

1 teaspoon paprika

2 bay leaves, crushed

swordfish kabobs

2 lb/1 kg swordfish fillets, cut into 1 1/4-in/3-cm cubes

12 whole bay leaves

2 lemons, thinly sliced, plus lemon wedges, to serve

2 green bell peppers (capsicums), seeded, deribbed and cut into 1 1/4-in/3-cm squares

16 firm, ripe cherry tomatoes

Salt and freshly ground pepper

seafood medley

6 lobster or crayfish tails

12 fresh clams, soaked overnight

12 large shrimp (prawns),
in their shells

12 mussels, scrubbed and soaked

12 baby octopus

12 oysters

12 sea scallops

1 cup/8 fl oz/250 ml olive oil

6 garlic cloves

Salt and black pepper

Lemon wedges, to serve

Cut lobster tails in halves. Prize clams open and remove top shell. Slit through shrimp shells along backbone and remove intestinal vein. Prepare a fire in a grill to a high heat. Arrange seafood on a grill rack and sprinkle with olive oil. (Octopus and crayfish tails should take about 10 minutes; mussels, clams and shrimp, 5–6 minutes; scallops and oysters, 2 minutes. Discard any mussels that do not open.) Transfer to a large platter when cooked and keep warm.

Mash garlic well and place in a mixing bowl. Slowly add olive oil, whisking briskly to a smooth, thick emulsion like mayonnaise. Season to taste. Serve seafood with garlic mayonnaise and lemon wedges.

SERVES 6

lemon and garlic marinade

Lemons and seafood have a natural affinity. This delicious marinade can be used for a whole fish, for fillets, and also in seafood salad dressings or on mixed leaf salads.

Place 4 sprigs fresh mint, 3 large cloves garlic and a 1-in/2.5-cm-wide spiral of lemon zest (rind) in a sterilized glass jar.

Add 4 cups/32 fl oz/1 l white wine vinegar to cover the ingredients in the jar completely.

Seal the jar and let stand in a warm, bright area for about 10 days (but not in direct sunlight) before using. Store in a cool, dark place— will keep for about 2–3 months.

grilled shrimp
with mango salsa

2 cups/16 fl oz/500 ml olive oil

8 cloves garlic, thinly sliced

Juice of 2 limes

1 teaspoon salt

$1/2$ teaspoon freshly ground
black pepper

2 lb/1 kg large shrimp (prawns),
peeled and deveined (20–24 shrimp)

Lime wedges, to serve (optional)

mango salsa

2 ripe mangoes

6 green (spring) onions, including
tender green tops, thinly sliced

2 fresh jalapeño chilies, stemmed,
seeded (if desired) and finely diced

2–3 tablespoons coarsely chopped
fresh cilantro (fresh coriander/
Chinese parsley) leaves

Juice of 2 limes

1 teaspoon salt

Soak bamboo skewers in water for 30 minutes. Heat olive oil in a frying pan over medium heat. Add garlic and cook, stirring occasionally, for 3–5 minutes, or until soft. Remove from heat, pour into a shallow non-aluminum dish and let cool. Add lime juice, salt and pepper. Mix well.

Thread 4 or 5 shrimp onto each skewer, passing the skewer through points near both the head and tail sections of each shrimp. Place skewers in olive oil marinade, turning to coat evenly. Marinate, covered, in the refrigerator for 2–12 hours.

Peel mangoes and cut flesh from pits. Cut into $1/4$-in/6-mm dice and place in a bowl. Add green onion, chilies, cilantro, lime juice and salt. Stir to mix, cover and refrigerate salsa for at least 30 minutes before serving.

Prepare a fire in a grill. When hot, place skewers on grill rack about 3 in/8 cm from coals and grill, turning once, for about 3 minutes per side, or until shrimp turn pink and are opaque throughout.

Make a bed of salsa on each plate and top with a skewer of shrimp, or remove shrimp from each skewer and arrange on salsa. Garnish with lime wedges, if desired, and serve.

SERVES 4–6

shrimp skewers

marinade

1 tablespoon fresh lemon juice

2 tablespoons fruity Italian white wine

2 tablespoons olive oil

8 lemon zest (rind) strips, each about 2 in/5 cm long

1/2 teaspoon crumbled bay leaf

1 teaspoon fresh thyme leaves or 1/2 teaspoon dried thyme

3 large cloves garlic, minced

Freshly ground pepper

shrimp skewers

1 lb/500 g jumbo shrimp (prawns), peeled and deveined (12–16 shrimp)

1 lb/500 g zucchini (courgettes), trimmed and cut lengthwise into slices 1/8 in/3 mm thick (12–16 slices)

6–8 paper-thin slices prosciutto, cut lengthwise into halves

bruschetta

8 slices country-style white bread, each about 1/2 in/1 cm thick

1 large clove garlic, cut in half

4 teaspoons olive oil

garnish

Small fresh thyme sprigs

with bruschetta

 Combine all marinade ingredients, including pepper to taste, in a shallow non-aluminum bowl, and stir well. Add shrimp to marinade and turn to coat. Cover and refrigerate for at least 4 hours, or overnight.

Soak 4 bamboo skewers in water to cover for 30 minutes. Remove shrimp from refrigerator about 30 minutes before cooking time.

Prepare a fire in a grill. Arrange zucchini slices on a grill rack and grill for 3 minutes. Turn over and continue to cook for 2–3 minutes longer, or until limp. Set aside to cool. Maintain the charcoal fire.

Remove shrimp from marinade, reserving lemon zest strips. Drain skewers. Wrap 1 piece of prosciutto around center of each shrimp, then wrap with a zucchini slice. Thread 3 or 4 wrapped shrimp onto each skewer and garnish each skewer with 2 of the reserved lemon strips.

Arrange skewers on a grill rack over hot coals. Grill shrimp for 3–4 minutes, turn over and continue to cook for 2–3 minutes longer, or until pink and slightly curled.

While shrimp are cooking, toast or grill the bread, turning once, until golden on both sides. Rub a cut side of the garlic clove over one side of each warm bread slice; brush with 1/2 teaspoon of olive oil.

Arrange bruschetta and skewers on a platter or divide among individual plates. Garnish with thyme sprigs and serve at once.

SERVES 4

salads and dressings

No barbecue is complete without good crusty bread and a few fresh salads. For entertaining that's free of fuss, make your salads a couple of hours ahead, cover with plastic wrap (film) and refrigerate. Bring them to the table just as the meat comes off the grill to keep them crisp and appetizing and let your guests help themselves.

mixed herb salad
with garlic dressing

garlic dressing

Salt

1 head garlic, separated into cloves,
peeled and thinly sliced

3/4 cup/6 fl oz/190 ml olive oil

1/4 cup/2 fl oz/60 ml fresh lemon juice

1 teaspoon sea salt

1/2 teaspoon freshly ground pepper

mixed herb salad

1 large bunch fresh flat-leaf (Italian) parsley,
about 4 oz/125 g, stemmed

1 large bunch fresh mint, about 4 oz/125 g, stemmed

2 bunches watercress,
about 10 oz/315 g total weight, stemmed

 Bring a small saucepan three-fourths full of water to the boil and add salt to taste. Add garlic and parboil for about 3 minutes to soften slightly and mellow the flavor. Drain and let cool.

Place cooled garlic in a small bowl and add oil, lemon juice, sea salt and pepper. Whisk to dissolve sea salt and form a dressing.

Combine parsley, mint and watercress in a salad bowl. Drizzle dressing over greens and toss to coat evenly. Serve immediately.

SERVES 4–6

mixed leaf salad

12 oz/375 g mixed lettuce leaves, such as mignonette, butter lettuce, green oakleaf, spinach, arugula (rocket) and radicchio, washed and dried

dressing

1/4 cup/2 fl oz/60 ml olive oil

1 tablespoon tarragon vinegar

1 teaspoon Dijon mustard

Salt and freshly ground black pepper

couscous tabbouleh

1 cup/8 oz/250 g instant couscous

1 cup/8 fl oz/250 ml boiling water

3 large tomatoes, peeled, seeded and finely chopped

1³/₄ oz/50 g finely sliced green (spring) onions

2–3 tablespoons finely chopped fresh mint leaves

2 oz/60 g finely chopped flat-leaf (Italian) parsley

dressing

¹/₃ cup/2¹/₂ fl oz/80 ml fresh lemon juice

2 tablespoons olive oil

1 teaspoon salt

Place couscous in a large bowl. Pour on boiling water and stir thoroughly. Set aside until couscous has absorbed the water.

Combine all dressing ingredients in a small bowl and whisk thoroughly.

Combine tomatoes, green onions, mint and parsley in a large serving bowl. Stir couscous with a fork to separate grains and break up any lumps. Add couscous and toss all ingredients thoroughly. Pour on dressing and mix again thoroughly.

Serve at room temperature, or chilled.

SERVES 6

Combine all salad leaves in a large serving bowl. Tear any larger leaves into pieces of a manageable size.

Combine all dressing ingredients in a small bowl and whisk thoroughly. Pour dressing over salad, toss thoroughly and serve immediately.

SERVES 6

speedy salad ideas

You can use any leftover grilled meat or chicken as the basis for a quick and easy salad the next day. Dress up the meat with a tasty mayonnaise or chutney. Serve with a simple salad dressed with a quick-mix vinaigrette. Here are some ideas.

minted coconut chutney

This chutney complements the flavor of grilled beef or lamb.

Chop 1 1/2 oz/45 g fresh mint leaves finely in a food processor. Remove. Place 1 medium onion, cut into fourths, in the food processor and chop to a smooth paste. Add 1 oz/30 g flaked unsweetened coconut, 1/4 teaspoon black mustard seeds (optional), 1/4 cup/ 2 fl oz/60 ml white wine vinegar, 2 tablespoons sugar and salt to taste. Process until well mixed. Spoon into a serving bowl and stir in the mint.

mustard mayonnaise

Serve this with thin slices of grilled beef.

Combine 1/4 cup/2 fl oz/60 ml mayonnaise, 1 tablespoon Dijon mustard, 2 teaspoons Worcestershire sauce and a few drops of Tabasco sauce in a small bowl. Whisk together until well blended.

peanut sauce

Cold grilled chicken and peanut-flavored sauce make a great team.

Heat 1 tablespoon olive oil in a pan over medium heat. Add 1 finely chopped onion and 1 minced garlic clove. Cook for a few minutes until the onion is soft. Add 1 tablespoon curry powder, 1 tablespoon brown sugar, 1 tablespoon soy sauce, juice of 1/2 lemon, 2 teaspoons white wine vinegar, 1 teaspoon hot chili sauce, and 1/4 cup/2 fl oz/60 ml dry sherry, stirring well to combine. Simmer over low heat for 5 minutes. Add 1/2 cup/4 oz/125 g crunchy peanut butter and 1 cup/8 fl oz/ 250 ml coconut milk and stir until well combined. Simmer over low heat for about 3 minutes, or until the sauce thickens slightly. Cover surface of sauce with plastic wrap (film) and allow to cool to room temperature. Just before serving, spoon over sliced chicken.

pasta salad

salad

6 1/2 oz/200 g fine tagliatelle pasta

6 1/2 oz/200 g Belgian endive (chicory/witloof), washed and finely shredded

1 head/3 1/2 oz/100 g radicchio, washed and finely shredded

3 oz/90 g Gruyère cheese shavings

1/2 large red bell pepper (capsicum), finely sliced

dressing

2 tablespoons lemon juice

1/4 cup/2 fl oz/60 ml light olive oil

2 tablespoons light (single) cream

1 tablespoon mayonnaise

2 tablespoons snipped fresh chives

Salt and pepper

greek salad

dressing

¹/₂ cup/4 fl oz/125 ml good-quality olive oil

2–3 tablespoons fresh lemon juice

3 tablespoons dried oregano

Freshly cracked pepper

1 clove garlic, finely minced (optional)

salad

2–3 cups/2–3 oz/60–90 g torn assorted salad greens of your choice

4 small ripe tomatoes, cored and cut into wedges

1 large cucumber, peeled, seeded and cut into wedges

1 red (Spanish) onion, thinly sliced into rings

2 small green bell peppers (capsicums), seeded, deribbed and thinly sliced crosswise into rings

8 oz/250 g feta cheese, coarsely crumbled

20 Kalamata olives

To make the dressing, combine olive oil in a bowl with lemon juice, oregano, cracked pepper to taste, and the garlic, if using. Set aside.

Combine greens, tomatoes, cucumber, onion and bell peppers in a large salad bowl. Drizzle the dressing over the top and toss gently. Sprinkle feta cheese and olives over the top and serve.

SERVES 4

with creamy dressing

Cook the tagliatelle in boiling salted water until al dente. Run under cold water and drain. Set aside until cold.

Combine all salad ingredients with pasta in a large mixing bowl.

Combine all dressing ingredients in a small bowl. Whisk together thoroughly. Pour dressing over salad and toss well.

Serve at room temperature.

SERVES 4–6

summer vegetable salad

Bring a large pan of salted water to the boil. Add broccoli, bring back to the boil and simmer over moderate heat for about 5 minutes, or until broccoli is tender. Drain and refresh in cold water. Repeat for squash, shortening the cooking time.

Place carrots in a saucepan, cover with cold water, bring to the boil and simmer over moderate heat for several minutes, or until tender. Refresh in cold water. Drain.

Combine all vegetables in a bowl. Toss with dressing and serve.

SERVES 4

1 1/2 lb/750 g broccoli, cut into florets

11 oz/345 g yellow squash (marrow), quartered

2 carrots, peeled and cut into thick matchsticks

1 red bell pepper (capsicum), cut into strips

vinaigrette

1 1/2 tablespoons grainy mustard

1/4 cup/2 fl oz/60 ml tarragon vinegar

Salt and freshly ground pepper

3/4 cup/6 fl oz/190 ml good-quality olive oil

bean salad
with japanese dressing

Bring a pan of salted water to the boil. Add beans and cook for 3 minutes. Plunge into cold water, drain and set aside to cool.

Combine wasabi and water in a screw-top jar. Blend and let stand for 5 minutes. Add remaining ingredients and shake vigorously to blend.

Toss beans with dressing and serve.

SERVES 4

* Wasabi powder is very hot, so use less the first time you make this dish if you are not familiar with its spicy flavor.

1 lb/500 g "yard-long" (snake) beans

1 teaspoon wasabi powder*

2 teaspoons water

2 tablespoons rice vinegar

1 garlic clove, finely chopped

1 teaspoon sesame oil

1 teaspoon soy sauce

1 tablespoon sesame seeds, toasted

rice salad
with summer squash

About 1/2 cup/4 fl oz/125 ml olive oil

5 assorted small summer squashes, such as zucchini (courgettes), yellow crookneck or straightneck, or pattypan, in any combination, trimmed and cut into 1/4-in/6-mm dice

Salt and freshly ground pepper

1 yellow onion, diced

2 cloves garlic, minced

2 teaspoons ground cumin

2 tablespoons distilled white or cider vinegar

2 cups/14 oz/440 g steamed rice, cooled to room temperature

4–5 tablespoons coarsely chopped fresh parsley

Chopped lettuce leaves

Heat 2 tablespoons olive oil in a frying pan over high heat. Add a third of each type of squash and season to taste. Cook, stirring often, for 1–2 minutes, or until lightly browned and slightly soft. Transfer to a bowl. Cook remaining squashes, in 2 more batches, in the same way, using 2 tablespoons oil with each batch. Let squash cool.

Heat remaining 2 tablespoons oil over medium heat in the same frying pan. Add onion and cook for 3–5 minutes, or until lightly golden. Stir in garlic and cook briefly. Add cumin, reduce heat to low and cook for about 2 minutes longer. Add to bowl holding squash. Add vinegar, rice and parsley and toss to mix well. Taste and adjust seasoning. (At this point, the salad can be covered and refrigerated for up to 3 days. Bring to room temperature before serving.)

To serve, line individual plates with lettuce leaves and spoon salad on top.

SERVES 4–6

arugula salad
with parmesan

Combine arugula leaves, Parmesan cheese and black pepper in a large serving bowl.

Combine all dressing ingredients in a small bowl and whisk thoroughly.

Pour dressing over salad and toss thoroughly. Serve immediately.

SERVES 6

2 bunches arugula (rocket), washed and dried

1³/4 oz/50 g Parmesan cheese shavings

Freshly ground black pepper

dressing

1/4 cup/2 fl oz/60 ml walnut oil

1 tablespoon tarragon vinegar

warm salad
of mushrooms and asparagus

Clean mushrooms with a damp cloth. Halve any large ones. Cut asparagus into 2-in/5-cm lengths and cook in boiling salted water until just tender. Plunge into cold water. Drain.

Heat walnut oil in a large wok or frying pan. Add button and shiitake mushrooms and stir-fry for 2 minutes. Add oyster mushrooms and stir-fry for 2 minutes. Add asparagus and stir to combine. Season to taste.

Arrange watercress on a serving plate. Pile mushrooms and asparagus in center.

Bring raspberry vinegar to a boil in the pan used for the mushrooms. Pour vinegar over salad and serve.

SERVES 6

3¹/2 oz/100 g shiitake mushrooms

5 oz/155 g button mushrooms

5 oz/155 g oyster mushrooms

1 bunch/5 oz/155 g asparagus

1/4 cup/2 fl oz/60 ml walnut oil

Salt and freshly ground pepper

1 bunch/3¹/2 oz/100 g watercress, washed and dried

2 tablespoons raspberry vinegar

grilled eggplant roll-ups
with goat cheese

1 eggplant (aubergine)

Salt

Olive oil, for brushing

Freshly ground pepper

3–4 tablespoons chopped
fresh chives

3 cloves garlic, minced

Balsamic vinegar, for sprinkling

Leaves from 12 fresh thyme sprigs,
finely chopped, or 1 tablespoon dried
thyme, crumbled

1 log/7 oz/220 g fresh goat cheese,
at room temperature

 Cut off and discard a thin slice from each end of eggplant. Cut eggplant into lengthwise slices ¼ in/6 mm thick. Lay slices on a double thickness of paper towels and sprinkle generously with salt. Let stand for about 20 minutes, or until beads of water appear on the surface. Rinse with cold running water to remove salt and bitter juices, then pat dry with additional paper towels.

Prepare a very hot fire in a grill. Brush eggplant slices lightly on one side with olive oil and place on grill in a single layer, oiled sides down. Brush tops with extra oil and grill for about 2 minutes, or until eggplant begins to soften and grill marks are clearly visible; turn and grill for about 2 minutes more, or until soft but not too deeply browned. Using tongs, transfer slices to a large platter as they are done.

Arrange half of the slices in a single layer on another platter and sprinkle with salt and pepper to taste. Scatter half of both chives and garlic evenly over slices and sprinkle with a little balsamic vinegar. Sprinkle thyme evenly over the top.

Top with remaining eggplant slices, again in a single layer, and scatter remaining chives and garlic over top. Sprinkle with a little more vinegar. Let stand in a cool place for at least

flavored vinaigrettes

With a little imagination, you can introduce intriguing flavor notes to your salads by including herbs or aromatic vegetables and fruits in your basic oil-and-vinegar salad dressings. Here are a few suggestions:

tomato vinaigrette

Peel, seed, drain and finely chop 1 medium tomato. Place in a screw-top jar with 1/2 cup/4 fl oz/125 ml good-quality olive oil, 2 tablespoons apple cider vinegar, 2 teaspoons honey, 1 clove garlic, minced, 1 teaspoon soy sauce, 1/4 teaspoon paprika, salt to taste and a dash of Tabasco. Shake until well combined. Keeps for 1 week in the refrigerator. Especially good with egg salad or artichokes.

dill vinaigrette

Warm 3/4 cup/6 fl oz/190 ml good-quality olive oil in a small saucepan. Crush 1 teaspoon dried dill with your fingertips and add to oil. Add 1/4 cup/2 fl oz/60 ml champagne vinegar and salt and pepper to taste and mix well. Keeps for 1 week in the refrigerator. Especially good with a potato salad or watercress and smoked trout.

anchovy vinaigrette

Combine 1/2 cup/4 fl oz/125 ml good-quality olive oil with 2 tablespoons wine vinegar, 1 tablespoon rinsed and finely chopped anchovies, 1 tablespoon finely chopped parsley and black pepper to taste. Shake well. Keeps for 1 week in the refrigerator. Especially good with grilled vegetables.

honey-mustard vinaigrette

Combine 1/4 cup/2 fl oz/60 ml honey with 1 cup/8 fl oz/250 ml good-quality olive oil, 1/2 cup/ 4 fl oz/125 ml wine vinegar and 2 tablespoons lemon juice in a small bowl. Stir in 2 tablespoons of mild prepared mustard and season with salt and pepper to taste. Whisk until thick and smooth. Keeps for 1 week in the refrigerator. Especially good with a green salad, potato salad or egg salad.

2 hours, or cover and refrigerate for up to 3 days.

When ready to serve, carefully spread each eggplant slice with goat cheese and roll up. Secure with a toothpick, if desired. Serve at room temperature.

SERVES 4–6

desserts

When it comes to the last course for a barbecue, you may prefer to prepare a cool dessert ahead of time or simply serve bought or homemade ice cream or a colorful fruit salad. Here are a few suggestions of the make-ahead kind, but don't forget how fabulous a platter of caramelized fruit can be straight off the coals (see page 92).

strawberry delight

3 cups/24 fl oz/750 ml
heavy (double) cream

1¹/₂ cups/12 oz/375 g
strawberries,
roughly chopped

³/₄ cup/3 oz/90 g toasted
slivered almonds

9 amaretti cookies,
crushed

¹/₃ cup/3 fl oz/100 ml
brandy

3 egg whites

³/₄ cup/6 oz/185 g
superfine (caster) sugar

¹/₂ teaspoon baking
powder

Whip cream and set aside. Mix strawberries, almonds and crushed amaretti in a bowl with brandy. Set aside for 10 minutes. Beat egg white until stiff and soft peaks form. Slowly add sugar and baking powder, and beat until shiny. Fold egg white and strawberry mixture into cream, working it in lightly but thoroughly. Pour into individual serving dishes or a patterned mold, and freeze, covered, for 4–5 hours (depending on size of container).

SERVES 6

ginger-peach sorbet

4 ripe peaches, peeled,
pitted and cut in chunks

2 tablespoons fresh
lime juice

2 tablespoons sugar

1 egg white

4 pieces sweet stem
ginger in syrup or
crystallized ginger,
chopped

Process peaches, lime juice and sugar to a smooth purée in a food processor fitted with a metal blade. Pour into a shallow metal pan and freeze for about 2 hours, or until edges are firm and center is soft.

Beat egg white in a large bowl until almost stiff; set aside. Return partly frozen peach purée to food processor and process for about 30 seconds, or until frothy. Add ginger and egg white to processor and, using on-off pulses, process for 3–5 seconds, or just long enough to blend in the egg white.

Pour mixture into a freezer container, cover tightly and freeze for 1–2 hours, or until firm but not frozen solid. Allow to soften (season) for about 30 minutes in the refrigerator before serving.

SERVES 4

summer berry pudding

1 loaf day-old white bread, crusts removed (about 15 slices)

1½ cups/12 oz/375 g raspberries

1 cup/8 oz/250 g red currants

1½ cups/12 oz/375 g blackberries

1½ cups/12 oz/375 g blueberries

¾ cup/6 oz/185 g superfine (caster) sugar

¾ cup/6 oz/185 g strawberries, sliced

Heavy (double) cream, to serve (optional)

 Line a medium-size bowl with bread, reserving enough to make a lid. Combine raspberries, red currants, blackberries, blueberries and sugar in a saucepan. Cook over moderate heat for about 8 minutes, or until juice starts to run. Remove from heat and add strawberries. Pour into bread-lined bowl and cover top with reserved pieces of bread. Lay a piece of plastic wrap over top and place a plate over this. Weigh down the plate with 2 cans or similar heavy weight. Refrigerate for at least 24 hours. Turn out onto a plate and serve with cream, if desired.

SERVES 8

tiramisù

5 extra-large egg yolks

5 tablespoons/2¹/₂ oz/75 g sugar

1²/₃ cups/13 oz/410 g mascarpone cheese, chilled

1³/₄ cups/14 fl oz/440 ml heavy (double) cream, chilled

¹/₄ cup/2 fl oz/60 ml brewed strong espresso coffee, at room temperature

¹/₄ cup/2 fl oz/60 ml coffee-flavored liqueur

24 good-quality chocolate or plain ladyfinger biscuits

Raspberries (optional)

Dutch processed cocoa

 Using an electric mixer set on high speed, beat egg yolks in a bowl with sugar for 5–7 minutes, or until pale yellow, smooth and shiny. Add mascarpone and beat for 3–4 minutes, or until thickened and smooth. Using clean beaters or a whisk, whip cream in another bowl until soft peaks form. Using a rubber spatula or whisk, fold whipped cream into mascarpone mixture until thoroughly blended, breaking apart any lumps.

Combine espresso coffee and liqueur in a small bowl. Arrange biscuits in a single layer over bottom of a decorative serving bowl 10 in/25 cm in diameter. Brush a little of the coffee mixture evenly over biscuits. Turn biscuits over and brush again until they are almost soaked. If using raspberries, arrange around edge. Spoon some mascarpone mixture over biscuits to make an even layer about ¹/₂ in/1 cm thick. Place remaining biscuits in a single layer over mascarpone mixture and brush tops with remaining coffee mixture. Arrange more raspberries around edge. Spoon remaining mascarpone mixture on top, smoothing to cover completely. Cover and chill for at least 6 hours, or up to 2 days, before serving.

Using a fine-mesh sieve, sift a light dusting of cocoa over the top. Using a large serving spoon, scoop portions of tiramisù onto individual plates.

SERVES 8

cream-filled apricots

Soak apricots in a bowl in water to cover overnight. Drain.

Combine sugar and 2 cups water in a saucepan over medium heat. Bring to a simmer, stirring to dissolve sugar. Simmer for about 10 minutes, or until thickened. Add apricots and cook for about 20 minutes, or until tender. Stir in lemon juice and continue to simmer for 1 minute longer.

Using a slotted spoon, transfer apricots to a baking sheet or large plate, reserving syrup in pan. Let cool enough to thicken slightly. If syrup is not thick, reduce it a little over medium heat.

If using whole apricots, carefully cut each apricot along the natural line with a small, sharp knife and remove pit to create a pocket. Using a small spoon or a pastry bag fitted with a plain tip, spoon or pipe *kaymak* or other filling into each pocket.

If using apricot halves, spoon *kaymak* or other filling on centers of half of them. Top with remaining apricot halves.

Arrange apricots side-by-side on a serving platter. Spoon thickened syrup over stuffed apricots and refrigerate until syrup is set, about 30 minutes.

Bring stuffed apricots to room temperature and sprinkle with pistachios to serve.

SERVES 4–6

8 oz/250 g whole dried Turkish apricots or dried apricot halves

1½ cups/12 oz/375 g sugar

2 cups/16 fl oz/500 ml water

2 teaspoons fresh lemon juice

1 cup/8 fl oz/250 ml *kaymak* (cultured cream), or 1 cup/8 oz/250 g crème fraîche or mascarpone cheese

2 oz/60 g chopped unsalted pistachios

wine-poached
peaches

6 yellow- or white-fleshed peaches

1 bottle/24 fl oz/750 ml fruity white or red
wine or Champagne

1/3–2/3 cup/3–5 oz/90–155 g sugar

1 vanilla bean (pod), split lengthwise

Bring a saucepan three-fourths full of water to a boil. Dip peaches into boiling water, one at a time, for 5 seconds each. Lift out with a slotted spoon and, using a sharp paring knife, peel peaches. Halve each along the natural line and remove pits.

In a saucepan large enough to hold all the peaches in a single layer, combine wine, sugar and vanilla bean. Heat gently, stirring until sugar dissolves. Taste and add enough extra sugar to achieve a pleasant sweetness. Bring to a simmer, add peaches and simmer for 2–5 minutes, depending on ripeness, or until barely tender.

Transfer peaches and cooking liquid to a deep glass bowl (peaches should be completely covered by liquid) and cool to room temperature. Cover tightly with plastic wrap and refrigerate for at least 2 days, or up to 3 days.

Using a slotted spoon, transfer peach halves to large wine glasses, placing 2 halves in each glass. Half-fill each glass with poaching liquid and serve.

SERVES 6

caramelized fruit

A platter of caramelized fruit, served simply with thick cream, yogurt or ice cream, makes a great finale.

Choose firm, ripe peaches, plums, apricots, figs, bananas or slices of pineapple. Halve fruit and peel, if necessary, allowing 3 or 4 pieces per person, depending on the size of the fruit. Arrange fruit of your choice, either one kind or mixed, on a hot grill plate and cook until browned with nice grill marks on one side. Sprinkle with brown sugar and continue to cook, turning pieces, until sugar bubbles and caramelizes. Remove to a large platter or individual serving dishes and serve with ice cream, thick cream or yogurt. If you wish, you can stir a little honey through the yogurt and spice it with a dash of ground cinnamon.

apricot trifle
with berries

Make jelly according to directions on package. Refrigerate until set, then chop roughly. Cut cake into slices, spread with jam, sprinkle with sherry and set aside. Place berries and apricot halves in a bowl and toss until combined.

Scald 3 cups/24 fl oz/750 ml of the milk in a saucepan. Combine remaining milk with the cornstarch to form a smooth paste. When milk is hot, stir in sugar and salt until dissolved. Add cornstarch mixture and stir well. Cook this custard, stirring constantly, over low heat until mixture boils and thickens. Add some of the custard to the eggs to warm them. Add eggs to custard and cook, stirring, for 3 minutes, or until eggs are cooked and the custard coats a spoon. Pour custard into a bowl, whisk in vanilla. Place a sheet of plastic wrap on custard to prevent a skin from forming and chill.

To assemble trifle, arrange half the cake slices over base of a very large serving dish (or 2 large dishes), top with half the custard, then half the jelly and half the berries and apricots. Repeat these layers, finishing with a layer of fruit. Refrigerate overnight. At serving time, decorate trifle with whipped cream. This dessert is best made 1 day in advance.

SERVES 20

3/4 cup/6 oz/185 g strawberry or raspberry jelly crystals

2 small store-bought or homemade sponge or plain yellow cakes

1 1/4 cups/13 fl oz/410 ml strawberry jam

1 1/2 cups/12 fl oz/375 ml sweet sherry

1 cup/8 oz/250 g strawberries, hulled and halved

2 cups/16 oz/500 g blueberries

2 cups/16 oz/500 g raspberries

1 cup/8 oz/250 g fresh apricot halves

4 cups/1 qt/1 l milk

1/2 cup cornstarch (cornflour)

2/3 cup/5 oz/150 g sugar

Pinch of salt

6 eggs, lightly beaten

2 teaspoons vanilla extract (essence)

Whipped cream, for decoration

coffee ice

2¹/₂ cups/20 fl oz/625 ml hot brewed espresso
or brewed French- or Italian-roast coffee

About ¹/₃ cup/3 oz/90 g sugar

¹/₂ cup/4 fl oz/125 ml half-and-half (half cream) or milk

Unsweetened whipped cream, to serve

Chocolate shavings, to serve

Combine the hot coffee with sugar to taste in a 2¹/₂-qt/2.5-l stainless-steel bowl and stir until the sugar is completely dissolved. Add half-and-half or milk and mix well. Refrigerate until cold; place, uncovered, in the freezer.

After 30–40 minutes, when ice crystals have started to form around edges, whisk mixture vigorously to blend in crystals. Return bowl to freezer and whisk again every 20–30 minutes until mixture is a mass of coarse ice crystals, yet still soft enough to spoon (2–3 hours total). (If ice becomes too hard in the freezer, stand at room temperature for a few minutes, then whisk to the correct consistency.)

Divide ice among small serving bowls. Top each serving with whipped cream and chocolate shavings.

SERVES 4–6

stuffed figs

¹/₂ cup/2¹/₂ oz/75 g slivered blanched almonds,
plus 12 whole blanched almonds

¹/₄ cup/2 oz/60 g sugar

2 oz/60 g semisweet chocolate, chopped

12 large dried figs

vanilla ice cream
with strawberries

2 cups/16 fl oz/500 ml vanilla ice cream

1¼ cups/10 oz/315 g strawberries, stems removed, halved lengthwise

¼ cup/2 fl oz/60 ml balsamic vinegar, or to taste

1 tablespoon sugar

Coarsely ground pepper, to taste

Remove ice cream from freezer and let stand at room temperature for 10–15 minutes, or until it is soft enough to stir into the strawberries.

Meanwhile, in a bowl large enough to accommodate the ice cream eventually, stir strawberries with balsamic vinegar, sugar and pepper to taste. The vinegar and sugar will mix with the berries' natural juices to create a sauce. Taste and add more vinegar if needed.

When ice cream is soft enough, add it to berry mixture. Immediately stir together until berries and ice cream are evenly distributed. Spoon into tall wine glasses and serve at once.

SERVES 4

Preheat oven to 350°F/180°C/Gas Mark 4. Spread slivered and whole almonds on a baking sheet, keeping whole nuts separate. Bake for 8–10 minutes, or until toasted and fragrant. Cool. Set aside whole almonds. Leave oven at the same setting.

Combine sugar, slivered almonds and chocolate in a food processor fitted with a metal blade. Using rapid on-off pulses, process to a coarse paste.

Using a small, sharp knife, cut off fig stems, then cut a small slit 1-in/2.5-cm deep in top of each fig. Using a small spoon, stuff each slit with about 1 teaspoon of almond-chocolate mixture. Pinch openings closed. As figs are stuffed, place them on a baking sheet, stem-side-up.

Bake for 5 minutes. Turn figs over and continue to bake for about 5 minutes longer, or until softened. Remove from oven and press a whole almond into each slit. Serve warm or at room temperature.

SERVES 6

index

Acknowledgments

Weldon Owen would like to thank the following people: Sarah Anderson, Lisa Boehm, Trudie Craig, Janine Flew, Peta Gorman, Michael Hann, Aliza Pinczewski, Puddingburn Publishing Services (index)

Photographs and recipes on pages 3, 6 (top and center), 7, 12-13, 16, 19, 21, 23, 24-25, 28-29, 30, 31, 32-33, 35, 36-37, 38, 39 and 61 appear courtesy of Meat and Livestock Australia.

Photography Mark Burgin, John Callanan, Kevin Candland, Rowan Fotheringham, Mike Hallson, John Hollingshead, Peter Johnson, Allen V. Lott, Ashley Mackevicius, Joyce Oudkerk Pool, Penina, Alan Rosenberg, Chris Shorten, Rodney Weidland

Styling Janice Baker, Jan Berry, Penny Farrell, Carolyn Feinberg, Kay Francis, Heidi Ginter, Stephanie Greenleigh, Consuelo Guinness, Jane Hann, Susan Massey, Jacki Passmore, Pouké, Vicki Roberts-Russell, Suzie Smith